portrait of a leader

tim **elmore**

a guide for emerging leaders

contents...

I would like to offer special thanks to my interns from the summer of 2000 who devoted their time to the production of this book. Sarah Conley (Taylor University), Paul Hoyt (Liberty University), and Erin Moss (Anderson University). And to Janise Matyas who brought this book to completion. Their work is greatly appreciated.

Well, you did it. You have yet another book in your hand, as though you needed something else to read and consume your time. But wait. This one is different. We tried to create something that didn't just beg you to read it and then forget it.

This book is designed to guide you into understanding leadership better than you ever have before. The way we plan to accomplish this feat is to invite you into discussion with a small group of others who are on the leadership journey with you. This book will simply provide the platform for loads of discovery and discussion on leadership.

There are four principles we want you to recognize before you jump in to it:

1. First, becoming a leader is a process not an event. As Christians, we tend to overestimate the importance of events and underestimate the importance of process. As you read and write in the pages of this guidebook, don't rush it. The eight chapters are designed to be completed in sixteen weeks, or about one semester. We suggest you take two weeks per chapter and really discuss and pray about each one. In order to facilitate this, we have indicated a good breaking point in each section by marking it "HALF TIME."

2. Second, you'll get the most out of the chapters if you reflect and respond to the interactive sections. Each chapter provides places for you to "talk back" and share what you think. Grab a pen every time you pick this up and write down your personal responses to the truths of each section.

3. Third, don't work through this guidebook alone. It is designed to be discussed in a small group. We like to call them "mentoring groups" because you will be mentored both by the content of the workbook as well as the pooled thoughts of each member of your group. Listen and share. God speaks through the most unlikely people.

4. Fourth, this particular guide covers only one dimension of leadership. The entire set consists of six books, all created to be used in small mentoring groups. The book series will cover 1) the spiritual formation of a leader, 2) the skill formation of a leader, and 3) the strategic formation of a leader. Be sure to digest the material and study the scriptures that go with it. By the time you finish all the books, you will have covered most everything you need to embrace in order to lead others well.

Remember, leadership is a noble calling. There is nothing wrong with the desire to be a more effective influence on others around you, unless it is for selfish reasons. The Apostle Paul wrote: "Therefore, knowing the fear of God—we persuade men." This should be our attitude as well. Jesus already called you the "salt of the earth." He was speaking of our influence on the world around us. It's time we live out this calling effectively.

I have already prayed for you. I pray for everyone who gets their hands on this book. May God bless you as you seek to bless others…as a healthy, effective spiritual leader.

Dr. Tim Elmore
EQUIP

One more thing...

There will be sections in each chapter that are highlighted with various symbols. Below is a key detailing what these symbols mean.

 A Scripture passage or story follows. You will probably want to grab your Bible for this section of the book.

 This is a real life scenario or a story given to help clarify the point and bring it to life.

 At this point in the book, you will have a chance to reflect and respond to the content as it relates to your life. This is an interactive workbook, so when you see this symbol, pick up a pen, think about the questions asked, and jot down what comes to mind.

 Following this will be important insights or significant truths you won't want to miss – so be sure to pay attention to the content that follows this symbol.

 This symbol indicates a main point or the "bottom line" of a chapter. In a simple paragraph is summarized the essential truth(s) that we want you to walk away with.

 To make sure you are not missing anything, there will be sections where you will have a chance to review where you have been and what you have learned.

 This indicates key truths presented to you in a simple list format

 At the end of every chapter is a section for you to assess yourself. This gives you a chance to see where you are in light of what you have just read, and to incorporate the truths of the chapter into your life.

 We have suggested that you take two weeks per chapter and really discuss and pray about each one. This bar will appear in the middle of the chapter to indicate a good stopping point.

My prayer for you…

Next to your decision to follow Jesus Christ, your decision to lead and influence others is the most significant one you will make in your life. It will have a ripple effect that could continue long after you are gone. Sociologists tell us that the most introverted people on earth will influence 10,000 other people in an average lifetime. Just think how many your life might impact! My prayer is for you to become a student of leadership for life. May this book be a guide on your journey.

God never calls a wrong number

how God calls a leader

In the late 1800's, a group of young job seekers congregated in the waiting room of a telegraph hiring agency. Each job prospect who was waiting for an interview was engulfed in reading, chatting and munching . . . except one young man. Through all the commotion he heard a message tapped out in code, "If you hear this message come through the office door." With ears perked up, the man understood the invitation being offered. So the young man walked through the office door. A few minutes later he returned to the waiting room, grinned and told the other job seekers, "You can all go home, I just got the job."

Like the prophet Isaiah (Isaiah 6.1-8), this young man heard the general call that went out to everyone in the waiting room, and responded to it, making it his call. He listened. He understood. He acted. He got results.

wrong number?

Wrong numbers are dialed millions of times each day across the U.S. But how do you know it's a wrong number? What's your first clue? Have you ever thought about how you draw the conclusion that they have the wrong number?

1. First, you don't recognize the other person's voice.
2. Second, they ask for someone you don't recognize.
3. Third, the subject they bring up doesn't make sense or seem relevant to you.

Often when God calls us, we are tempted to treat it like a wrong number for the same reasons. His call seems strange. It feels like it is for someone else. But it is not! As a result of this lesson, many of us will realize that God has placed a call on our lives that we must respond to, now. A call to serve is a call to prepare.

the fact of the matter...

You can lead now! God often calls us as young people to serve, and we don't have to wait to make a major impact on our world. Remember 1 Timothy 4.12 "Don't let anyone think less of you because you are young, but be an example . . . " (NLT)

BASIC TRUTH

You will become what you are becoming right now.

God's got your number...

In the Bible, we see at least four different ways that God "called" people into their life-purpose. His calling unfolded just like it does for ordinary people like us today:

thunderbolt –
EXAMPLE: APOSTLE PAUL

This is the call that we all pray for—it's unmistakable. It's a thunderbolt. Paul experienced this call as he was on the road to Damascus. God spoke, the bright light shone, and Paul's life was changed forever. These calls often occur at a crisis event in a moment or a season of our lives when we suddenly know what to do. It might happen in a service or one night when we're praying and our lives are changed for eternity. However it occurs, the call comes clearly.

walking through open doors –
EXAMPLE: QUEEN ESTHER

This call comes over time. It is a progressive revelation, one step at a time. Esther, the queen of Persia in the Old Testament, simply made wise, God-honoring decisions that eventually saved her fellow Jews from annihilation. She was a beautiful Jewish girl that was picked as queen in a foreign land. She earned influence with the king and built relationships with those around her. While she was queen, Mordecai her mentor, discovered a conspiracy against her people. Esther responded by simply obeying God and taking the steps of opportunity along the way. They didn't seem big at the time and her call didn't make sense until it all came together in the end.

call from birth –
EXAMPLE: JEREMIAH

Those whom God has called from birth have known their calling ever since they can remember. (They might not have responded to the call, but they know that they've been called). When Jeremiah was only a young man, God called and informed him that he was going to tear down nations and setup other nations. Jeremiah told God that he was too young for the work. Yet God reassured Jeremiah of His intentions: "Before you were born I set you apart and appointed you as my spokesman to the world (Jeremiah 1.5, NLT)."

growing awareness –
EXAMPLE: JOSEPH

This kind of call comes early, but only in a very general way. Those who have a growing awareness of their calling begin to understand that something is happening and start sifting through it early on in life. Even though they know "something's there", they don't fully comprehend what God has for them until they mature. Unlike "walking through open doors," when his call came, Joseph understood the "big picture" up front, as a teenager. What he didn't understand were the detail. He realized them along the way. Joseph began his life with a leadership dream (the early sense of a call), then he was sold into slavery and thrown into prison. All of this led up to his being put second in command of Egypt. As you read about Joseph's life in Genesis, you realize that he had a growing awareness that God was fulfilling the dream as he matured, filling in the details along the way.

6

reflect and respond...

Have you ever experienced God's call on your life? If you don't believe that you have, you will learn more about it through this chapter. If you have been called, describe the experience below. What evidence have you seen to reinforce the call? Can you identify with any of the four ways God called people in scripture?

David's life...

King David, the man after God's own heart, was called to lead a entire nation while he was still in his teens. Although he was the least likely of his family to be crowned as king, God chose to call him anyway. And David led God's people to unprecedented spiritual and military prosperity.

Read 1 Samuel 16.1, 6-13. In this passage, we get to look in on David's call from God and his anointing by the prophet Samuel.

from the book...

"The Lord said to Samuel, 'How long will you mourn for Saul, since I have rejected him as king over Israel? Fill your horn with oil and be on your way; I am sending you to Jesse of Bethlehem. I have chosen one of his sons to be king.'

"When they arrived, Samuel saw Eliab and thought, 'Surely the Lord's anointed stands before the Lord.' But the Lord said to Samuel, 'Do not consider his appearance or his height, for I have rejected him. The Lord does not look at the things man looks at. Man looks at the outward appearance, but the Lord looks at the heart.'

"Then Jesse called Abinadab and had him pass in front of Samuel. But Samuel said, 'The Lord has not chosen this one either.' Jesse then had Shammah pass by, but Samuel said, 'Nor has the Lord chosen this one.' Jesse had seven of his sons pass before Samuel, but Samuel said to him, 'The Lord has not chosen these.' So he asked Jesse, 'Are these all the sons you have?'

"There is still the youngest' Jesse answered, 'but he is tending the sheep.' Samuel said, 'Send for him; we will not sit down until he arrives'. (It's at this point that Jesse retrieves his son David. Can you see the anticipation? Doesn't this scene remind you a bit of Cinderella and the glass slipper that doesn't fit her sisters?)

"So he went and had him brought in. He was ruddy, with a fine appearance and handsome features. Then the Lord said, 'Rise and anoint him; he is the one.' So Samuel took the horn of oil and anointed him in the presence of his brothers, and from that day on the Spirit of the Lord came upon David in power. Samuel then went on to Ramah ."
I Samuel 16.1-13 (NIV)

david's call...

We learn three important truths from David's call. These truths can also impact us.

I. God chose David to be a leader even when others put "lids" on him.

His dad didn't even ask him to come in from the field to be considered.

The first time it happened, David's father put a lid on David.

"Then Samuel asked, 'Are these all the sons you have?' 'There is still the youngest," Jesse replied, 'But he's out in the field watching the sheep . . .'" (1 Samuel 16.11, NLT)

Even Jesse, David's own father, was saying, "You're too young. You're just a shepherd. You just don't seem tough enough."

His brothers rebuked him when he visited them on the battlefield.

Eliab, David's brother, was the second person to place a lid on him.

"But when David's oldest brother, Eliab, heard David talking to the men, he was angry. 'What are you doing here anyway?' he demanded. 'What about those few sheep you're supposed to be taking care of? I know about your pride and dishonesty. You just want to see the battle!'" (1 Samuel 17.28, NLT)

Eliab was telling David, "You can't help us. You're too young and irresponsible for us. We're too busy for you."

King Saul didn't believe in him and thought he could only succeed with the king's armor.

If it wasn't hard enough on David to have his own family not believe in him, even the king of the entire nation didn't believe that he could succeed on his own.

"'Don't be ridiculous!' Saul replied, 'There is no way you can go against this Philistine. You are only a boy, and he has been in the army since he was a boy!' Then Saul gave David his own armor—a bronze helmet and a coat of mail."

Saul was basically saying to him, "You're too young. Goliath is experienced. If you do go, do it my way in my armor. It's your only hope of survival." (1 Samuel 17.33,38, NLT)

Goliath thought he was a joke and never took him seriously.

Not only did David's friends put a lid on his ability, but also his enemies.

"Goliath walked out toward David . . . sneering in contempt at this ruddy-faced boy. 'Am I a dog,' he roared at David, 'that you come at me with a stick?' And he cursed David by the names of his gods. 'Come over here, and I'll give your flesh to the birds and wild animals!' Goliath yelled." (1 Samuel 17.41-44, NLT)

Goliath mocked David by saying he looked young, fair, and "soft." He taunted him and then cussed him out!

Have others ever told you that you couldn't do something even though you believed that you could . . . Or not even offered an opportunity to you because they didn't believe that you could handle it . . . Or not taken you seriously despite the fact that you believed God had called you to what you were going to attempt? Describe how they placed a lid on you.

2. God looked at David's heart and knew his faith and passion were genuine.

Not only do we see that God chose David to be a leader even when others put "lids" on him, we also see that God looked at his heart and knew his faith and passion were genuine.

David's faith was in God, not his own abilities.
David had seen God's faithfulness demonstrated in previous times of his life, so he had faith that God would continue to be faithful.

"The Lord who delivered me from the paw of the lion and the paw of the bear will deliver me from the hand of this Philistine." (I Samuel 17.37, NIV)

David's passion was for God's Kingdom, not his own.
David didn't desire to take the challenge of fighting the Philistine to prove his abilities or to prove to Israel that he was a leader. Instead, he realized that Goliath was defying God, and someone needed to do something about it.

"David said to Goliath, 'You come to me with sword and spear and javelin, but I come against you in the name of the Lord Almighty, the God of the armies of Israel, whom you have defied.'"
(I Samuel 17.45, NIV)

David's vision was to make God known to the world.
When David saw Goliath, he didn't just see the challenge, he saw how God could gain glory by the situation.

"This day the Lord will hand you over to me...and the whole world will know there is a God in Israel." (I Samuel 17.46, NIV)

David's heart was like God's heart.
Early in his life, David cultivated intimacy with God. When he was only a youth, God purposely chose him as king because of his godly heart.

"...the Lord has sought out a man after His own heart, and appointed him leader of His people..." (I Samuel 13.14, NIV)

reflect and respond ...

If God were to search your inmost being—your deepest thoughts, motivations, and desires—would He describe you as a person after His own heart? The answer to this question is one of the most crucial factors in spiritual leadership. Whether you are going into ministry or not, desiring God's glory is still a vital part of your leadership. Leadership accomplishments without God are simply wood, hay, and stubble. Although they may gain you notoriety, success, and wealth on earth, they are not a part of God's ultimate plan. Would God consider you a person after His own heart? Write what characteristics would make you this kind of person.

3. God called David as a teen for the same reasons he calls us today.

David was fifteen when he was anointed King of Israel. He must have felt inadequate. Most of us at fifteen years old are only concerned about fitting in and not embarrassing ourselves. Many of us have wondered at some point: "Why would God call me to be a leader? What do I have to offer? I'm no Billy Graham. I still feel like a kid who's trying to figure out who God is and where my life should go. Besides, it's not like the whole world is following me now anyway. I have more questions than answers."

This is exactly why God wants to use us. We can be molded. We are dependent upon Him. We know we can't do it by ourselves. We don't have the money, brains, network, power or confidence to try it on our own.

David was only one of many young leaders God called early in life:

David's early call in life is not an exception to the way that God works. God also called some of the great leaders in the Bible (as well as many of the greatest leaders throughout history) at an early age.

1. JEREMIAH: JEREMIAH 1.4-7

Jeremiah was God's spokesman to Judah. For forty years he boldly and courageously proclaimed God's message to God's people. But he was called and he began his public ministry at a young age.

"The Lord gave me a message. He said, 'I knew you before I formed you in your mother's womb. Before you were born I set you apart and appointed you as my spokesman to the world.'

"'O Sovereign Lord,' I said, 'I can't speak for you! I'm too young!' 'Don't say that,' the Lord replied, 'for you must go wherever I send you and say whatever I tell you. And don't be afraid of the people, for I will be with you and take care of you. I, the Lord, have spoken.'" (NLT)

2. SAMUEL: 1 SAMUEL 3,1-10

Samuel was called while he was still a boy serving in the temple

After Hannah gave her son to the Lord, Samuel grew up in the Temple. Eli taught him, as a young child, everything he should know about serving the Lord.

3. JOSIAH: 2 KINGS 22,1-2

Josiah became king when he was only 8 years old! And he is remembered for obeying God completely in his leadership.

"Josiah was eight years old when he became king, and he reigned in Jerusalem for thirty-one years...He did what was pleasing in the Lord's sight and followed the example of his ancestor David. He did not turn aside from doing what was right." (NLT) (Josiah was used by God to purge Israel of idolatry when he was only 20 years old!)

4. TIMOTHY: 1 TIMOTHY 4,12

Timothy was one of Paul's closest companions, and he was called to be a church leader while he was still young.

"Don't let anyone think less of you because you are young. Be an example to all believers in what you teach, in the way you live, in your love, your faith and your purity." (NLT)

5. JESUS' DISCIPLES: MATTHEW 4,21-22

God called James and John at an early age to follow him. These two disciples, along with Simon Peter, made up Jesus' inner circle of friends.

"A little farther up the shore he saw two other brothers, James and John, sitting in a boat with their father, Zebedee, mending their nets. And he called them to come, too. They immediately followed him, leaving the boat and their father behind." (NLT)

Consider why God might have called David as a teen:

1 HIS WHOLE LIFE WAS IN FRONT OF HIM.
He would have years in his future to make an impact for God.

2 HIS FAITH AND ZEAL WERE HOT, UNLIKE OLDER GENERATIONS.
He was willing to attempt the impossible for God—not just the conventional.

3 HE WAS TEACHABLE & AVAILABLE AS A SHEPHERD WATCHING THE SHEEP.
He had time to worship and listen to God—and learn from Him as he waited.

4 HE WOULD GIVE GOD ALL THE GLORY SINCE HE WAS INEXPERIENCED.
He knew he was young and inexperienced, so victory would belong to the Lord.

rewind <<<

Reflect on your own life. Why might God call you now, while you are still young?
List specific reasons. How do you think that answering God's call on your life will change it? In the next section we will look at why we should respond to God's call.

**God's perspective
1 Timothy 4.12**
"Don't let anyone think less of you because you are young. Be an example to all believers in what you teach, in the way you live, in your love, your faith and your purity."

(NLT)

why we should answer God's call to become a leader.

So, even if God has called us to be leaders, why should we answer His call? Four reasons compel us to pick up the phone and answer God's call to become a leader.

because every generation must reach their own generation for Christ

Christianity is always one generation away from extinction. No one can reach our generation as effectively as we can. Each time God raises up a new generation of disciples, He commissions them to reach their own generation. We must become students of leadership because there's a world we must lead to Jesus.

real life...

During the days of the Apostle Paul—Asia Minor was the center for the Christian faith. It was the Bible belt of ancient times. He had planted churches all over that area. If we went there today, we would find present day Turkey—a hotbed for Islam. Why? The generations who followed Paul did not reach their own generation.

As late as three centuries ago, Europe was the center for Christianity. No longer. Europe is spiritually dry and decaying. Why? The generations who followed did not reach their own generation. But how about our generation? It's our turn now!

reflect and respond...

We all have people that God placed within our sphere of influence that we can best impact and reach. Who have you established a relationship with that God wants you to reach? How will you reach them?

because we will influence others whether we want to or not

Secondly, we must answer God's call because we have influence over others. Sociologists tell us the most introverted of people will influence 10,000 others in an average lifetime. Think about it. No matter how shy we are, we will rub off on 10,000 people before we die—and that's not even trying! And if we're a leader—even in little ways, how many might we influence? 50,000? 100,000?

On a scale of one to ten, we may never feel like a "ten" as a leader. Maybe we only feel like a "four". But don't you think we could grow from a "four" to a "seven", by studying leadership and becoming more effective as a leader? This is why we must study leadership. We must leverage our influence the best way possible for the King.

real life...

A boy named Trevor Ferrell founded Trevor's Place in Philadelphia, PA. At age 11, Trevor was watching the news when a story came on about the homeless in Philadelphia. He spoke to his parents that night, and they agreed to pray about the need—but he knew that wasn't enough. He talked them into going downtown and giving a blanket and sack meal to a homeless person. That began a journey, over the last seventeen years that now employs several staff, has a location in the city and provides food and warmth to hundreds of homeless people in Philadelphia.

because the world needs leaders now more than ever

The third reason we must answer God's call is because the world needs leaders now more than ever. In recent times, many different leaders in varying leadership roles have failed.

political	business	athletic	church
Presidents have been indicted for immoral and illegal conduct while in office.	CEO's have a high rate of suicide because of the pressure to perform and the desire for more money.	Athletes have become primadonnas driven by money, fame, and drugs.	Televangelists, pastors, and other church leaders have fallen into sexual sin and monetary

real life...

Just prior to the dawn of the 21st century, George Barna wrote: "After fifteen years of digging into the world around me, I have reached several conclusions regarding the future of the Christian church in America. The central conclusion is that the American church is dying due to lack of strong leadership. In this time of unprecedented opportunity and plentiful resources, the church is actually losing influence. The primary reason is the lack of leadership...Nothing is more important than leadership."

**God's perspective
Matthew 5.13-14**
"You are the salt of the earth. But what good is salt if it has lost its flavor? Can you make it useful again? It will be thrown out and trampled underfoot as worthless. You are the light of the world—like a city on a mountain, glowing in the night for all to see."

(NLT)

**God's perspective
2 Corinthians 5.11**
"It is because we know this solemn fear of the Lord that we work so hard to persuade others."

(NLT)

because when God starts a movement, he often goes to young people

The final reason we must become leaders is because God often starts movements with young people. Throughout the ages, God has raised up young people to accomplish what He could only do through their excitement, passion, and unquenchable spirit.

impacting the world...

JESUS' DISCIPLES

Jesus disciples were probably the same age as many of us. John was likely in his **late teens** when Jesus called him. He lived well into the 90s A.D. Jesus chose them because they would be willing to passionately follow Him and pull off the impossible.

THE HAYSTACK MOVEMENT

The haystack movement began when **students** were on their way to a church meeting one night. It began to rain, and they took cover under a haystack. When the thunderstorm grew worse, they decided to hold their own prayer meeting—and out of that meeting came a movement of missionaries that changed the world at that time.

THE CAMBRIDGE SEVEN

Ever heard of the Cambridge Seven? Less than 150 years ago, in the 1860s, seven **students** at Cambridge University in England decided to meet together to pray and discuss the needs of the world around them. They were especially burdened by China. From those seven students came a movement of workers that impacted China by the end of the nineteenth century.

THE STUDENT VOLUNTEER MOVEMENT

At the end of the 19th century, Christians felt the same urgency that we did at the end of the 20th century. They wanted to finish the task of world evangelism. Men like John Mott and Dwight Moody traveled around to **college campuses** compelling students to surrender their lives to the cause of the Great Commission. It was called the Student Volunteer Movement. Before the movement was over, more than 100,000 students stood up to be part of it by giving, praying and going. More than 30,000 actually went overseas—and packed all their belongings in a pine box. They knew that they would likely die early, and this box would serve as their casket.

OPERATION MOBILIZATION AND GEORGE VERWER

George Verwer was **18 years old** when God burdened him with the Great Commission. He knew he had to do something as a student at Moody Bible Institute. He took a team of other students to Mexico to serve there and to enable his friends to catch a vision for the world—and that began the ministry we call Operation Mobilization today. Hundreds of thousands of people have been impacted by the tens of thousands of missionaries they have sent out. It all started with a student.

JOHN WESLEY

John Wesley began his "Holy Club" when he was only a teenager. By the age of **seventeen** he founded the organization that developed into Methodism.

CHARLES SPURGEON

Charles Spurgeon was a well-known pulpit orator at sixteen. He was only **21 years old** when he became pastor of the Metropolitan Chapel where he spoke to crowds of 10,000.

GEORGE WILLIAMS

George Williams was **twenty-three** when he founded the Y.M.C.A.

JOHN CALVIN

John Calvin was just **seventeen** when he entered the pastorate.

BILL BRIGHT & CAMPUS CRUSADE FOR CHRIST

Bill Bright, who has been one of the most influential Christian leaders of our time, was a **student** being mentored by Henrietta Mears, at Hollywood Presbyterian church. One night, he spent most of the night praying, feeling as though God was calling him to reach the UCLA campus. Miss Mears asked: Why stop with just that campus? Why not the rest of the nation? From that challenge, Campus Crusade for Christ began, and at last count, CCC has reached **one billion** people for Christ around the world. Students have done most of the work!

what makes a great leader?

A leader is many things and each person has a unique style. These men who were great Christian leaders throughout history had very different personalities and styles of leadership from each other. Let's take a look at some other great characteristics of leaders.

EVERY GREAT LEADER IS A . . .

FUTURIST – their dreams are bigger than their memories.

LOBBYIST – their causes outlive and out speak their critics.

CATALYST – they initiate movement and momentum for others.

SPECIALIST – they don't try to do everything, but contribute in one area.

OPTIMIST – they believe in their cause and their people beyond reason.

ECONOMIST – they marshal every resource as a sacrificial steward of the cause.

ACTIVIST – they are "doers" and empower other people to unleash their potential.

STRATEGIST – they shrewdly plan how they can best harness and leverage their influence.

ENTHUSIAST – they have passion that defies logic, and they magnetically attract others.

PRAGMATIST – their legend is that they have solved practical problems people face.

INDUSTRIALIST – they are not afraid to roll up their sleeves and work long and hard.

FINALIST – they labor with diligence and devotion to the end; they finish well.

reflect and respond...

Which three roles are the easiest for you? Which three are the hardest? What will you do to develop the roles that don't come easily to you?

assess yourself...

After looking at how God has called young people throughout the ages to leadership, do you believe that God will use you to lead? This topic is easy to embrace in our minds but harder to grasp with our hearts—that we can lead now! We don't have to wait to make a major impact on our world! Judging by the way you live your life—your habits, time management, self-discipline, attitude—do you think that your life reveals God's call too?

What specific habits for better leadership can you begin to cultivate? For example, begin a personal growth plan by reading and listening to tapes, find a mentor, be more self-disciplined, change your attitude and speech, be a better time-manager, etc.

What vision has God placed within your heart? Where can you begin to make an impact RIGHT NOW! (Through campus leadership, through a non-profit organization, through community involvement, through an entirely new venture, etc.)

Commit to the Lord this plan of action. Ask him to give you the strength to take the leap into greater levels of leadership. Once you've prayed, sign your name and the date below to seal your commitment.

bringing it all home...

Find someone to keep you accountable to take the leap into greater levels of leadership. Ask them to encourage you as you begin this new challenge, whether it be your first leadership position or a greater leadership challenge.

Then tell as many friends, family, and others about your commitment so that you will have natural accountability.

"I pray that when I die, all of hell will throw a party to celebrate the fact that I am no longer in the fight."
— C. T. Studd

[primary colors]

the four essential qualities of effective leadership

Have you ever stopped and tried to define the essence of leadership? Is it filling a position? Is it doing a particular job? Is it having a certain identity? Our understanding comes most quickly when we have seen a "portrait" of a true leader – a snapshot from real life.

the real leader...

I heard a documentary about a very unlikely encounter between two Nebraska leaders. The first leader was Michael Weisser. Michael began to get involved in his community by asking neighbors what they thought the town needed. One common response had to do with the steadily growing ethnic population. There were lots of African-Americans, Hispanics and Asians moving into town and it was making the locals uncomfortable. This sparked an idea for Mike. He began offering welcome baskets to these new neighbors. His idea was an instant success and a team assembled to help him with the project.

The second leader in this documentary, was Larry Trapp, the local Grand Dragon of the Ku Klux Klan. Larry stood for everything contrary to what Michael was doing. In fact, he was also greeting new neighbors . . . he was seeking out these individuals and anonymously threatening their lives! Unhappy about Michael *welcoming* these same people, Larry promptly left a threatening message on his answering machine.

Since every call deserves a call back, Michael decided to leave Larry a voice message. "I got your phone call," he began, "and I just want you to know that I did a little homework on you too. I discovered that you are diabetic and confined to a wheelchair [both of these discoveries were true]. I just thought that someone like you could use the help of someone like me. You see, I have a van and I'd be happy to pick you up and run some errands with you. If you ever could use my help, just let me know."

Michael left messages for four weeks, but never caught Larry at home. When they finally connected, Michael assured him that the offer was still good. Larry was dumbfounded at first, yet he finally decided to take Michael up on the offer. For the next few weeks, the two men ran errands. One day, Larry finally asked Michael *why* he was helping him. Michael responded, "I'm trying to follow God as best I can. I'm just trying to do what I think God would do if He were here with you right now." Upon hearing this, Larry began to weep and shared his heart. Before the conversation was over, Larry was praying with Michael. His life would never be the same. For that matter, neither would the life of the community where they lived.

The story was splashed across the morning papers: "KKK Leader Gets Religion." Larry publicly apologized to the people he'd threatened in the article. He decided to join the basket ministry so he could personally take baskets to the people he had threatened. He ended up moving in with Michael and was mentored by him for a year and a half before Larry died from his diabetic complications. Yet it wasn't until the entire community was transformed, racially and spiritually. It all happened because one ordinary man decided to get involved and lead instead of playing it safe and minding his own business.

2

BASIC TRUTH

All effective leaders possess the four primary qualities of leadership: character, perspective, courage, and favor.

true leadership...

Notice the authentic leadership in this account. No titles, positions, or power was involved—only true leadership. Several observations may be made through the example of Michael Weisser.

True leadership . . .

- does not depend upon conferred authority, titles, positions or fame.
- can occur whenever a need emerges that sparks passion within someone.
- may take on a variety of methods, styles and appearances because the *outcome* is what is most important to the leader.
- works toward a breakthrough of impact or achievement.
- occurs when one person acts upon the vision of a preferred future and then mobilizes others to join in the cause.

reflect and respond...

What comes to mind when you hear the word leader? List six characteristics that make a good leader:

1.   4.

2.   5.

3.   6.

leadership is influence...

Even if we do not "feel" like leaders, we must realize that leadership can be summed up in one simple word: INFLUENCE. Influence is something that every person has. As I said in the previous chapter, sociologists tell us that even the most introverted person will influence 10,000 people in his or her lifetime! And if we are intentional about being leaders, think how many more people we will influence!

the common threads of great leaders...

three actions they take:	three atmospheres they make:
CAST VISION: Leaders possess and communicate a picture of their goals to others.	**SENSE OF DESTINY:** Leaders have a picture of what they want and feel destined to fulfill it.
IMPLEMENT STRATEGY: Leaders understand and implement steps toward reaching the goals.	**SENSE OF FAMILY:** Leaders promote an atmosphere of support and belonging; no one feels alone in the task.
EMPOWER PEOPLE: Leaders mobilize and equip people to join them in the cause.	**MILITANT SPIRIT:** Leaders possess a resolve to reach the goal whatever the cost or sacrifice.

As a leader, which of the three actions do you do most naturally? Are you a natural at casting vision, implementing strategy, or empowering people? Which do you struggle with? Which of the atmospheres do you create most easily when you lead? Do you have a strong sense of family, of destiny, or a militant spirit? With which do you struggle?

the leadership equation

The greatest master pieces in the world all began with a few simple primary colors. I remember when my art history professor in college brought in several beautiful masterpiece paintings. He described the unique details of each picture. Afterward, however, he reminded us, "All of these began with just four primary colors: red, yellow, blue, and white."

Just as an artist begins with just a few basic colors, there are basic "colors" that make up a healthy, effective leader. Let's begin by looking at the primary colors of leadership.

the primary formula...

Healthy, effective, leadership results from "mixing" the following:

CHARACTER	PERSPECTIVE	COURAGE	FAVOR
1. The leader's backbone	1. The leader's mind	1. The leader's will	1. The leader's heart
2. Discipline and responsibility	2. Vision and faith	2. Commitment and risk	2. People skills and charisma
3. Inward strength	3. Inward sight	3. Inward spirit	3. Inward savvy and skill
4. An ability to stand up	4. An ability to see ahead	4. An ability to step out.	4. An ability to soar above.
This is our infrastructure	This is our insight	This is our initiative	This is our influence

character
perspective
courage
+ favor
―――――――――
healthy,
effective
leadership

I. CHARACTER:

Enables the leader to do what is right . . . even when it is difficult.

The first primary color of leadership is character. Character is the foundation on which the leader's life is built. It all begins with character because leadership operates on the basis of trust. "The only thing that walks back from the tomb with the mourners and refuses to be buried is the character of a man. What a man is survives him. It can't be buried." J.R. Miller

Character works for a leader in four essential ways:

Character . . .

- communicates credibility
- harnesses respect
- earns trust
- creates consistency

reflect and respond...

Think of a leader you admire. How does his or her character communicate credibility, harness respect, create consistency, and earn trust?

the ingredients

Note the three ingredients for character listed on the bar to the left. Do you have those in place in your life? Which will need the most work?

real life ...

In the early days of American history, several men wanted to become president. One of these men was Aaron Burr. . . yet it was in his early days that he actually ruined his chances at becoming president. One day, he stepped up to address the congress and to present a bill that was very unpopular. A friend grabbed his coat and pulled him off the platform. "If you speak on behalf of this piece of legislation you will kill your chance to become president!" his friend whispered passionately. Aaron Burr simply looked down at the paper in his hand and asked, "But is this bill right?" After a moment of thought, his friend responded, "Well, yes I believe it is." Aaron Burr then said the now classic words: "Well, then, I would rather be right than be president."

steps for developing character...

Solid character does not just happen — it must be purposely developed. Below are six proven steps for developing fracture-resistant character. You can begin these now!

- Discipline yourself to do two things you don't like every week.
- Fix your eyes on a clear, specific purpose.
- Learn the "whys" behind God's commands.
- Interview a leader who has integrity: How did they build it into their life?
- Adjust and monitor your motives for why you do what you do.
- Write out the promises you've made. Take responsibility for all your actions and emotions.

reflect and respond...

How would you rate yourself on the character scale? For example:

- When you say you'll finish an assignment, do you always follow through?
- Do you only claim credit for work that you personally have done?
- Do you color situations to reflect how you want them to appear?

On a scale of 1 to 10 (ten being the highest), how solidly would you rate your character? Explain the rating you chose and evaluate what is keeping you from having a perfect "10" character.

Look at the list at the top of this page titled "steps for developing character." Which of those things can you make a part of you life as you strive to improve you character? How will you implement those steps?

leaders:

**see bigger
see before
see beyond**

required
ingredients for
perspective . . .

- Building and casting vision.
- Understanding reality beyond and before the people.
- Discerning the process and people needed to reach the goal.

2. PERSPECTIVE:

Enables a leader to see and understand what must happen to reach the target.

The second primary color for healthy, effective leadership is perspective. Jesus began His training of the twelve by working on their perspective. He worked on their vision and how they saw life. He knew if He could get them to think differently, He could get them to act differently.

Character is essential, but anyone can have good character. Perspective is the first quality that separates leaders from followers. Leaders think differently than followers. They envision differently than followers. They see beyond, they see bigger, and they see before followers do.

> "The primary difference between a follower and a leader is perspective. The primary difference between a leader and an effective leader is better perspective."
> Dr. Robert Clinton

Leaders see the big picture and the little process . . .

1. They first choose their Vision (What is the goal?).

2. They then choose their Venue (What is the strategy to reach it?).

3. Finally, they choose their Vehicles (What systems to use to move ahead?).

real life...

In 1982, Walt Disney World in Orlando, Florida finished work on the Epcot center. It was a marvelous park, and the date was set for the grand opening. Since Walt Disney had already passed away, the Disney executives asked his wife, Mrs. Disney, to cut the ribbon and say a few words. When the Master of Ceremonies called her up to the podium, he smiled and said, "Mrs. Disney- I just wished Walt could have seen this!" She smiled and responded by saying, "He did."

steps for developing perspective...

Anyone can develop perspective in their life if they choose to think differently. Below are six steps to help us enhance our perspective.

- Watch the news or read the newspaper and ask: What could be done to solve these problems? Choose a crisis and list solution steps you would take if you were in charge.

- Groom the optimist in you. Read and listen to positive books and tapes. Feed yourself with big ideas from great people.

- Write out your dreams. What would you attempt to do if you did not fear failure?

- Interview a visionary leader. How do they think? How do they perceive things?

- Identify one burden you've embraced. Set some goals to address it.

- Post photos, pictures and quotes that represent your goals and dreams in your room.

22

reflect and respond...

Write about a vision that you have for your personal life. What venue and vehicles will you choose to make your vision a reality? Discuss the goal, strategy, and systems...

rewind <<<

Our world tends to define leaders by their title or position but there is a deeper level of leadership than simply an office with a view. Describe what "true leadership" looks like. What qualities of "true leadership" do you recognize in your own life?

List three things that you will do this week to improve the character and perspective in your life.

"The primary difference between a follower and a leader is perspective. The primary difference between a leader and an effective leader is better perspective."

Dr. Robert Clinton

HALF TIME...continue the chapter next meeting

In the first part of our lesson, we learned what "real leadership" looks like. We've also established that just as an artist uses four primary colors, leaders have four primary qualities to live by. The first two were character and perspective. Let's take a look at the next two.

3. COURAGE:

Enables the leader to initiate and take the risk to step out toward a goal.

With only character and perspective, a leader may still lack action. Only courage enables a leader to step out and practice the vision they possess inside of themselves. The only measure of what we believe is what we do. If we want to know what people believe, we don't read what they write, we don't ask what they think, we just observe what they do. Our personal lives shrink or expand in proportion to our courage.

courage is...

- ...contagious.
- ...initiating and doing what you are afraid of doing.
- ...the power to let go of the familiar.

- ...vision in action.
- ...risking and seizing what is essential for growth.

courage includes . . .

- Making and keeping commitments.
- Building the capacity to take risks.
- Lobbying for a breakthrough in a cause.

real life...

My first big lesson in courage came when I was in college. On a TV episode of 20/20, I saw the four members of the heavy metal band, KISS. They boasted about the drugs, sex and money they had, laughing about their exploits in front of millions of teenagers. At that point, I prayed: "God, somebody ought to do something about them!" Suddenly, I felt the Holy Spirit prodding me. In fact, I sensed He was impressing me to go and share Jesus with the members of KISS! The idea scared me to death, but the more I tried to ignore it, the deeper the impression became.

The next fall, KISS came to town, and God opened up a door for me to talk to them. I found the hotel where they were staying, and talked to a maid about which room they were in. I spotted their bodyguard outside their door at midnight. When I asked if I could talk to Gene Simmons and the rest of KISS, he reminded me he was there to protect them from people like me. Then, I showed him my personal tracts I had created for the band, and requested he simply give them to the guys, and I would leave. He took the tracts, then suggested I wait around a while. He told me that after the concerts, the band usually visited the bar and had a little nightcap – at about 2:00 am. If I was willing to wait, I could talk to them.

I did wait, but not without a major battle with fear. I saw visions of worst-case-scenarios: getting cussed at, beat up and thrown out of the bar by those guys. Fortunately, I sat down, prayed, and God reminded me of why I was there. I ended up meeting all the members of KISS and shared Christ with everyone of them that night. My greatest take-away, however, was simply learning how much God wants to use ordinary people to do extraordinary ministry...if they can only get beyond their fears.

reflect and respond...

Do you consider yourself a couragous person? Write about the last time that you did something that required great courage.

> "Courage is the first of human qualities because it is the one which guarantees all others."
>
> Winston Churchill

steps for developing courage...

To improve your courage, do the following . . .

- Attempt something each week that you could not possibly pull off without God.
- Invite accountability regarding commitments and decisions you've made.
- Give an all-out commitment to a good habit for a set time.
- Interview a courageous person. What gives them their courage?
- Do the thing you fear the most and the death of fear will be certain.
- Force yourself to be a decision-maker and a responsibility-taker.

reflect and respond...

How do you tend to handle fear? Do you embrace it? Are stretching experiences a regular part of your life? Or have you retreated so far into your comfort zone that you don't ever feel fear? Write about a time in your life or leadership experience when you lacked courage.

In what area of your life do you need courage right now? How can you develop it in that area?

4. FAVOR:

Enables a leader to attract and empower others to join them in the cause.

Finally, a leader must display relational skills to mobilize people. Without favor, a person may reach a goal, but may fail to take anyone with them! Leaders, by definition, always have followers.

If we have character, perspective and courage, we will likely become an entrepreneur who attempts great things in our life. However, we may be acting alone. The entrepreneur often travels alone. Leaders always take others with them.

key elements...

COMMUNICATION –
Leaders must develop listening skills and the ability to share ideas convincingly.

MOTIVATION –
Leaders must mobilize others for mutual benefit and empowerment.

DELEGATION –
Leaders must share their authority, responsibility and ownership of the vision.

CONFRONTATION –
Leaders must have backbone and be able to resolve relational differences.

REPRODUCTION –
Leaders must be able to equip and train a team of people to accomplish the goal.

reflect and respond...

Which of the "key elements" of favor come easily to you? Which are the most difficult for you? Why?

real life...

When John Maxwell became the pastor of Skyline Church in 1981, he faced a formidable challenge. He followed the founding pastor, Dr. Orval Butcher, who had led the church for 27 years. Consequently, some of the congregation didn't like John Maxwell. He was replacing their hero. Several people displayed their displeasure during John's first year, particularly one man, Harry Mitchell. He wouldn't even talk to John. Fortunately, John had developed some marvelous people skills and decided he would love Harry until he responded to his leadership. He asked Harry to meet him for a special one-to-one appointment. When the two sat down, John simply asked Harry tell him a bit about Dr. Butcher. Harry lit up. With great enthusiasm he shared for 45 minutes about what a great leader Pastor Butcher was. (John had succeeded in getting him to talk!) After Harry finished, John smiled and said, "Harry, you're right. Pastor Butcher really is a great leader. I want you to know that I think you should continue loving him just the way you do right now." Then John paused. "But Harry, I have a question for you. After you love Dr. Butcher with all that love, if there is any love left over — could I have that?" Harry began to cry. He knew the game he had been playing. And that day Harry hugged his new pastor for the first time. From that time on, every Sunday, Harry would initiate a hug with his new pastor. Each time Harry would hug Pastor Maxwell he would whisper in his ear, "This is the love I got left over."

required ingredients for favor . . .

- Building personal charisma
- Building people skills
- Communication, motivation, delegation, confrontation, & reproduction

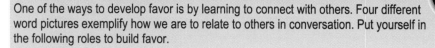

word pictures...

One of the ways to develop favor is by learning to connect with others. Four different word pictures exemplify how we are to relate to others in conversation. Put yourself in the following roles to build favor.

THE HOST:
Good hosts always take initiative and see to it that their guests are comfortable. We are to host the conversations and relationships of our lives.
How does a host take initiative and make you feel welcome in his/her home?

THE DOCTOR:
Doctors never give a prescription before first diagnosing the person by asking questions and examining them. We are to poke and prod with questions that inquire about other's interests.
How do you inquire inductively about other's interests with questions?

THE COUNSELOR:
Good counselors earn their right to speak by listening. We are to be an active listener, validating the other person.
How often do you take a break in your schedule to really listen to others?

THE TOUR GUIDE:
A tour guide is not hired to fellowship or be a buddy, but to get the people to their desired destination. We are to lead them through a process and get them to a destination.
How does a tour guide lead you on a journey? (Hint: the difference between a travel agent and a tour guide is that one of them goes with you!)

steps for developing favor...

Just like trade skills can be learned, our people skills can also be developed. But, unless our heart genuinely loves people, our skills can't effectively be developed because the result of this development will be manipulation not favor. But once our heart is right, our skills can greatly enhance our leadership.

- Learn to "host" the relationships and conversations you engage in.
- Determine to be others-centered, focusing on their needs, not on yours.
- Become a "good finder." Find one good quality in others and affirm it.
- Make deposits in the lives of people— encouragement, good books, tapes, contacts, etc.
- Identify the strengths in people and help them find a place to employ those strengths.
- Interview a people-person. How did they develop their charisma?

reflect and respond...

Find a friend and demonstrate each of the four word pictures in your conversation.
What can you say to become an effective host, doctor, counselor, and tour guide?

Fact

A leader has a compass in their head and a magnet in their heart.

what happens if I'm **missing a quality?**

Now that we've looked at different qualities that are part of effective leaders, let's look at what happens when one of these qualities is missing. In reality, it is unlikely that we have conquered each of these areas in our personal lives. It's important to recognize where our weaknesses are so that we can work on their improvement.

A leader must have all four qualities in order to perform over the long haul at an optimal level. We see this truth verified in the lives of those we read about in the pages of scripture. Notice what happens when just one component is missing from the equation.

perspective + courage + favor – character = SAMSON

Read Judges 13.24-16.31. Samson failed miserably because he didn't develop character. He knew right from wrong, possessed courage, and at times held favor and influence – but Samson never mastered character. He had strong biceps, but a weak backbone.

character + perspective + favor – courage = PILATE

Read John 18.28-19.16. Even if he possessed character, Pilate failed miserably. He may have had the right perspective and the power, but he failed to do what was right and risky due to lack of courage. He wouldn't take responsibility for the trial of Jesus, but rather washed his hands of it. Good leaders don't shirk responsibility.

character + courage + favor – perspective = SIMON PETER

Read Matthew 16.21-23. Peter displayed character and courage numerous times during Jesus' ministry and he seemed to have favor with his colleagues – but gaps in his perspective were clearly experienced. Sometimes Jesus even had to correct him in public!

character + perspective + courage – favor = JOSHUA & CALEB

Read Numbers 13.17-33. Caleb and Joshua came back from spying out the land with great perspective and courage, but they did not have enough favor to influence the people to move forward. Because they didn't have favor with the people, that generation was never persuaded to make it into the Promised Land.

reflect and **respond...**

All of us have different areas of strength and weaknesses. Which of these biblical characters do you identify with the most?

toxic leaders...

By comparing ourselves to past leaders we have a standard to evaluate ourselves against. If we realize the mistakes of other leaders, we can learn from them and avoid those same mistakes.

Leaders like **Nero**, **Adolf Hitler** and **Joseph Stalin** were destined to sabotage themselves. Nero possessed an enlarged ego that choked out his perspective. Hitler's lack of character choked out his perspective and favor. Stalin's character was so absent that he lost all favor with people and never got it back. These leaders' impact wound up being negative and short lived. They did not possess all the qualities of whole and healthy leaders. Toxic leaders often sabotage themselves because of several reasons.

TOXIC LEADERS TEND TO SABOTAGE THEMSELVES BECAUSE THEY HAVE . . .

- Too much **ego**
- Too much **insecurity**
- Too much **control**
- Too little **character**
- Too little **people skills**

assess yourself...

Review the four primary qualities of effective, healthy leadership. Do you exhibit these qualities in your life and leadership? As a leader, which of the four qualities of healthy, effective leadership are you strongest in? In which are you the weakest?

Looking back on the steps for developing the different qualities, write down specifically what you will do to enhance the quality that needs developing in your life.

bringing it all home...

A leader has been defined as one who knows the way, goes the way, and shows the way.

John Maxwell

(intimacy with God)

an intimate relationship with God is a leader's source and resource

When an Elvis Presley look-alike contest came to Massachusetts, the Boston Globe was on the scene. A story in the newspaper spotlighted a certain fan by the name of Dennis Wise. Listen to his comments . . . I think they are quite insightful:

> "Presley was and is my idol. I have seen his concerts, watched every movie he has done, I once got a hair contour like his, and now I have a face-lift . . . I have won Elvis look alike contests. I have every album he has recorded, I have ticket stubs and clippings from programs all over the world . . . I even have some Elvis pillows from Japan . . .
>
> "Often times I have wanted him to see me, so I would storm the stage, before and after the concerts he would do. It's funny; I don't think he ever noticed. I once even climbed the walls around Graceland, the Presley mansion. I think it might have been him wandering through the house as I looked through my binoculars, but I'm not sure. It's really funny, though. All the effort I put into following him . . . and I could never seem to get close."

There's an analogy in this article for you and me. How many times have we felt this way about our experience with God. We go to Bible Studies, pray, sing the songs and even lift our hands. Yet, if we are honest about it, we've all felt this way: it's funny...all the effort I put into following Him...and I could never get close.

intimacy...

Intimacy. People are talking about it more and more these days. Intimacy in marriages. Intimacy among friends. And, most of all — intimacy with God. We seek relationships that will fill our need for closeness. The ultimate relationship is one with God. People long to experience Him in a genuine way, and will follow leaders who create a place for it to happen. So, why don't leaders create a place for this to happen? Why is intimacy with God so hard to reproduce? Why do leaders struggle with this issue?

why leader's struggle with this issue...

- The idea of being intimate with God is mystical, ambiguous and subjective. It's hard to measure
- Our own personal intimacy with God is a struggle. We can't give what we don't have.
- We suffer from the common occupational hazards of ministry listed on the next page.

BASIC TRUTH

Your intimacy with God will impact your influence for God.

struggle... [continued]

Listed below are four "occupational hazards" that spiritual leaders often face. All of these hazards hurt our relationship with God. Although they are harmful, they are extremely easy to fall into. If we experience these hazards for more than a brief season of time, then we can begin to erode the foundation of our walk with our Father.

THE STARVING BAKER —

We're too busy providing bread for others to eat.

As a spiritual "baker," our life and schedule can become so consumed with " baking bread" for others that we don't have time or desire to feed ourselves. We begin to replace personal quiet time with God with preparation for Bible studies, worship times, or other ministries. The short-term result is that we feed others while starving ourselves. The long-term result is that we become so spiritually deficient that we lose the ability to even feed other people.

THE SUPERFICIAL CELEBRITY —

We keep others at a distance, including God.

We live in a culture of celebrities and stars. Even in Christian circles, the one up front is a "sage on the stage." Unfortunately, as a spiritual "superficial celebrity," we portray ourselves as unapproachable. We try to guard ourselves from being hurt, being manipulated, or being discovered as an imperfect leader. To maintain this masquerade, we must keep both God and others at a distance. We are never able to impact anyone else's life because we cannot allow them to get close enough to see through our superficial veneer.

THE POLISHED PERFORMER —

We're overly concerned with the "show" we do.

As spiritually "polished performers," we try to impress others with how spiritual we appear. As we become better at "playing the spiritual game," we appear to be deeper and may even be treated as spiritual leaders. In reality, however, we are far from that. If we perform long enough, we may find it hard to ever be genuine with God again. In the end, we suffer because of the distance in our relationship with God. Unfortunately, we often don't even notice what has happened because we are so caught up with our "show" on the platform.

THE SPIRITUAL PROFESSIONAL —

We perceive spirituality as our job.

As a spiritual "professional," we view our relationship with God and others as our job. Similar to the starving baker, we attempt to feed others something that we are not being fed ourselves. Those who are involved in ministry, whether as a lay person or as a pastor, are most susceptible to this. Our spirituality becomes a 9am to 5pm deal, or an "every Sunday" event where we try to turn on our relationship with God on demand. Since people expect us to be "spiritual," we fall into the trap of saying the right spiritual cliché at the right time to meet those expectations. Our life is no longer filled with genuine love for God, but rather with appropriate expressions of spirituality.

reflect and respond

Honestly evaluating our relationship with God can be both a painful and a rewarding experience. Take a minute and begin this workbook time with prayer. Ask God to give you the wisdom and the security to honestly pinpoint how intimate your relationship is with Him. Then ask Him to help you cultivate intimacy on a deeper level.

Now, which of these hazards have waylaid you along your spiritual journey? Describe a time when you have been a starving baker, superficial celebrity, polished performer, or spiritual professional…

in the beginning...

To get to the root of our dilemma, let's travel back to the book of Genesis. Adam was the first spiritual leader in the world. Scripture tells us he was to be the spiritual leader for Eve, his wife, as well as to take dominion of the earth and maintain the garden. When he sinned, the human race took on a new nature and bent toward independence. Their intimacy with God was shattered. It would require radical and reciprocal measures to recapture it again. This event was the beginning of the struggle for intimacy with God that we still face today. Note the impact of sin on mankind's intimacy with God. Our sinful nature causes us to…

1. Keep a distance from God
Instead of walking with God in the cool of the day, Adam and Eve hid from Him. Rather than pursuing their Creator with all of their hearts, they fled from Him because of their shame. Sin puts a chasm between God and us. We find it easier to be separated from God than pursue Him.

2. Disobey God
Our sinful nature causes us to desire independence from God and others. In the beginning, Adam relied upon God to set the agenda for his life. Adam's eating of the fruit was his first independent act apart from God. Today, we also desire independence from God. That is why it is so difficult to consistently make God's desires our desires.

3. Withhold our affections from God
Adam had the unique privilege of actually walking with God in a literal sense. He was truly able to experience God at the most intimate level. But after he chose to disobey, he was afraid of the repercussions. The first emotion Adam felt after he sinned was fear. The emotional intimacy which they had shared was now broken. For us, we will not risk intimacy either if we are afraid of rejection or indifference.

4. Avoid responsibility for our state
Now that Adam had something to hide from God, he was faced with the new desire to avoid taking responsibility for his actions. Blaming Eve and God for his actions further strained his intimacy with God. Both he and Eve blamed someone or something else for their behavior. Their shame led to blame.

reflect and respond ...

When was the last time you disobeyed God? Be honest . . . God already knows your sin. After your disobedience, what affections did you withhold from Him? After you realized your sin, did you take responsibility for your actions? Or did you avoid responsibility by placing blame on someone else or making excuses like, "That's just one of my weaknesses, or "It's no big deal . . . God will forgive me"? Discuss it.

common barriers to intimacy...

Living with this independent nature makes intimacy difficult and foreign to us – both in our vertical relationship with God and our horizontal relationships with each other. This opposition against God introduces a whole new set of barriers that frequently prevent us from experiencing an intimate relationship with God.

1. Unconfessed sin /Disobedience
2. Negative self-esteem and insecurity
3. Poor models of intimacy growing up
4. Unforgiveness
5. Driven spirit
6. Distrust

defining intimacy...

Intimacy with God can be difficult to understand because it often seems mystical, ambiguous and subjective. The best understanding of this relationship comes from several key thoughts throughout the New Testament. Intimacy with God can be defined as:

Deliberately drawing near to God to experience the PROMISE of Ephesians 3.18–19 and the COMMAND of Matthew 22.37, which results in the FRUIT of John 15.15–16.

squeeze your own juice...

Read Ephesians 3.18-19. What is the reward of intimacy with God?

Read Matthew 22.37. What is the responsibility of intimacy with God?

Read John 15.15-16. What is the result of intimacy of God?

outcomes of intimacy...

When we experience intimacy with God (or with anyone else for that matter), certain identifiable elements can be seen in the relationship. We often experience (or at least desire to experience) these elements in a close friendship, a dating relationship and within our family. These elements are what continually draw us to develop deeper bonds. Here are some outcomes of an intimate relationship.

1. **SECURITY** - I am loved unconditionally. I'm fully known without fear of rejection.

2. **SELF-WORTH** - I am important in this relationship. I offer something significant.

3. **SENSITIVITY** - I want to sense and meet your needs. I want to feel and think as you do.

4. **SHARING** - I want to spend time with you. I want to share experiences with you.

Who is someone that you experience this intimacy with? What intimate experiences characterize that relationship? Now compare this relationship to the one you have with God. What are the similarities? What are the differences?

myths about intimacy...

Intimacy with God is often a misunderstood concept. Here are six common myths. Write the word "yes" or "no" after you read each one, based on whether you've ever struggled with the lie.

THE FEELINGS MYTH

If I feel spiritual, I must be close to God.

Truth: Many people involved in the New Age Movement feel close to God, yet they are not truly intimate.

THE KNOWLEDGE MYTH

I know so much scripture, I must be close to God.

Truth: Even though atheists know Scripture, they do not experience intimacy with God. Jesus was more upset at the Pharisees than He was toward the prostitutes!

THE EMOTION VS. TRUTH MYTH

If I feel badly, I must not be intimate with God.

Truth: If our relationship with God were truly based on emotion, it would have been over long ago. King David felt horrible as he repented of his sin with Bathsheba, yet he was never closer to God than in that act of repentance.

THE GOOD DEEDS MYTH

If I work at doing good, I know I'm close to God.

Truth: Intimacy with God will not be achieved through accomplishing a spiritual checklist. Many claim that they are saved by grace, but they continue to cling to their righteous acts as if *they* are the justifying force for their acceptance.

THE POSITIONAL MYTH

Intimacy with God is automatic if I'm "in Christ."

Truth: Being in Christ is automatic if you're a Christian, but abiding in Him is not. There is a difference between our position in Christ and our abiding in Christ. Abiding is a day to day experience.

THE INTENSITY MYTH

If I serve God with great zeal, I must be intimate.

Truth: Believing that the intensity of our ministry dictates our intimacy level with God is a performance trap. Many people serve God on a short term mission trip and build a hospital. However, they may mistake intensity for God and intimacy with God.

Many times, these myths seep into our lives without us even knowing it. Slowly, they become foundational to how we relate to God. The more we embrace these myths, the more we put a lid on our capacity to be intimate with God.

We all want intimacy, yet we hide behind a smokescreen to prevent it from ever becoming a reality.

Which of these myths are evident in your walk with God? How have these lies affected your intimacy with God?

five levels of **intimacy...**

Obviously, we all experience different levels of intimacy with God and each other. Even during Jesus' ministry on earth, He watched people grow into various stages of intimacy with Him:

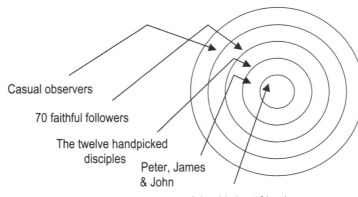

Casual observers

70 faithful followers

The twelve handpicked disciples

Peter, James & John

John, his best friend

Degree of Jesus' Interaction With Others

the stages of **intimacy...**

As we move toward intimacy (whether with people or with God), these general stages are encountered. We progress toward intimacy one-step at a time, as we feel safe.

1. **Cliché:** Phrases we use out of courtesy, but carry no risk or transparency.
   When we are least intimate with God, we simply speak to Him in cliché's. "Father, bless this food to our bodies . . ."

2. **Facts:** Growing closer by sharing information from our lives.
   We begin to share facts such as prayer requests for our health, car, or other concrete details in our life. "Father, my car needs a new muffler, and my parents are traveling . . ."

3. **ideas & opinions:** Sharing deeper the personal thoughts we have on issues.
   We progress to sharing with God our thoughts about things that happen around us. Father, please help Carrie not to get offended when I share with her . . ."

4. **Feelings:** Opening up to share our emotions, being vulnerable about who we are.
   We become more intimate, we even share our deep emotions with God. "Father, right now I'm hurting because . . ."

5. **total honesty:** Exhibiting the deepest level of trust by sharing our very life.
   When we reach the deepest level of intimacy, we become fully honest and transparent before God. "Father, I don't know why you have called me to do this, but I'm relying on you for everything . . ."

reflect and respond ...

Just as we experience these five steps in human relationships, we also experience them in our relationship with God. Discuss how you are experiencing these levels and stages of intimacy with God.

real life...

I met Adam in 1987, when I went to Budapest for a missions trip. In broken English, this nineteen year old communist soldier asked me why I was in his country. I explained that I had traveled with a team, hoping to share about our relationship with God and see if anyone was interested in knowing more about it. At this point, I discovered that Adam knew just enough English to cuss me out . . . he basically told me to take my religion back to America!

As soon as I got back to my tent, I caught my wife and said "Honey, we've got to pray for Adam. I am going to try to meet with him every day and I want to be able to share the gospel before I leave."

It was hard to communicate with him at first, but over the next three weeks, Adam and I spent nearly every day together. On the final night we sat around a campfire with the team, munching on popcorn. After finishing, Adam and I set off for our last walk.

"Adam," I started, "I feel like I need to apologize for coming on so strong these last three weeks with my Christian faith . . ." He interrupted me. "Oh no, you don't need to apologize at all. I have thought a lot about God since you have been here. In fact, I have talked to the air twice (this is what he called praying) and both times my requests were answered!"

For the next two hours we talked. At the end of the conversation I asked him, "what would keep you from inviting Christ to take over your life?" Through broken English, Adam said to me, "Well, if knowing God means having what you guys have, I want Him in my life."

a cross-cultural relationship...

This is a real life picture of why intimacy with God is so difficult. To go from hostility to friendship, Adam and I had to cross the bridges of unfamiliarity, language, world view and culture. It took three weeks, a lot of patience and much determination. Now consider this: our relationship with God requires work because it, too, is a cross cultural relationship. Think of the daunting gap between God and us! In Isaiah 55.9-11, He says, "my ways are not your ways, and my thoughts are not your thoughts." If it took so much work to build a friendship between Adam and me, how much more must we devote to God? One reason more people don't experience intimacy with God is that it is simply too much work. Cross-cultural relationships require effort!

rewind <<<

We have looked at why intimacy with God is essential to leadership. Do you agree? Why or why not? Which barrier is the number one hindrance in your relationship with God? Discuss it. Next we will look at how to cultivate this intimacy that is so vital.

God's perspective
Isaiah 55.8

"My thoughts are completely different from yours," says the Lord. "And my ways are far beyond anything you could imagine."

(NLT)

a t.h.e.o.l.o.g.y. for intimacy...

For us to become intimate with God, we need to take the necessary steps to understand the essential ingredients for it. It doesn't just happen – there are certain issues to be settled before we will experience an intimate relationship with Him. We will need to stir the following ingredients into the recipe and put ourselves into position to experience Him. Memorize this acronym for the word theology to remind you what will be needed.

t – TIME

We can't experience real closeness with anyone overnight. Time is often the most difficult essential to add. We must give Him time over the long haul. In other words, our relationship with God needs to be "crock-potted," not micro waved. We must daily spend time with God to develop an intimate relationship, over a lifetime.

APPLICATION: I must be patient

How much time do you spend with your Heavenly Father? Do you need to be investing more time? If so, how do you plan to make a change?

h – HUMILITY

Scripture says that God draws near to the humble but opposes the proud. He loves a broken and contrite heart; that is why *intimacy is always preceded by humility*. This is fleshed out in Jacob's life. God's wrestling match for control of Jacob's life began twenty years before the famous match in Genesis 32.22-31. God must break us of self-sufficiency, self-promotion, and self-righteousness. He manifests His presence in the holy place and the lowly place (Isaiah 57.15).

APPLICATION: I must be broken

Do you ever feel that you have wrestled with God as Jacob once did? Who won? Do you have a spirit of humility in your life?

e – EXPRESSION

We will not get close to God or to anyone else unless both parties express themselves in vulnerable, loving ways. Sometimes, it is easier to be more concerned with our image or reputation than in truly expressing our affection to Him with our words, actions, and song. Just as a husband doesn't shake hands with his wife, we should not be satisfied with trite and superficial expressions of love to God.

APPLICATION: I must learn to worship

How have you felt God expressing His love to you? How do you express your love for Him?

O - OPENNESS

God isn't found through rigidity or through keeping some sort of checklist. Rather, He is found through relational, honest and transparent approaches to His grace. This is illustrated in marriages. The couple does not pledge laws to each other, they pledge love.

APPLICATION: I must trust and be transparent

Do you feel that you are completely open with God? Is your heart a transparent place where there are no walls? If not, how can the walls be removed?

I - LISTENING

We must learn to listen to His voice if we desire intimacy. We don't lose intimacy when we stop talking to someone, but when we stop listening. Don't fall into the trap of substituting echoes of God for God Himself. We like to hear good tapes and good sermons, but only use these *after* you listen to Him personally! We must practice "wasting time" with God, as Richard Foster writes.

APPLICATION: I must invest time in prayer and Bible study

How often do you take time to really listen to God? What has He been saying to you lately?

O - OBEDIENCE

A desire to please and a willingness to act are pre-requisites to friendship. When we are friends with someone, we learn to love what they love. Jesus equated obedience and friendship. He said, "If you love me — you will obey me."

APPLICATION: I must act on God's requests

Is your desire to please God followed by actions of obedience? What recent steps of obedience have you taken in your life?

g - GRACE

God is not found by keeping the rules or performing for Him. Intimacy's foundation is love, not law. It is gratitude, not guilt. Just as loving parents come with open arms to their children after a spanking, so we must also realize that God always has His arms open to us . . . regardless of what we have done.

APPLICATION: I must let God love me...period

How have you experienced God's grace? What does grace look like in your own life? Do you find it easy to accept?

y - YEARNING

Intimacy doesn't happen automatically – we must desire it more that anything else around us! This yearning, hunger and passion for God is the most important factor in our intimacy.

APPLICATION: I must desire intimacy more than anything else in life

Do you find yourself yearning for God? How is your spiritual appetite right now?

reflect and respond...

These Biblical ingredients are necessary for us to experience passionate intimacy with God. Which of these ingredients do you need to cultivate the most? Specifically, how are you going to develop these elements?

Develop a plan for greater intimacy with God. When you're done writing the plan, you should be able to envision how this plan will help. (i.e. I will develop grace by practicing forgiveness of myself and others. I will also memorize a verse attesting to the grace of God every week for the next month. Etc.) Have an accountability partner keep you accountable to implement these actions.

A young man approached Socrates desiring to gain wisdom. He told Socrates he wanted wisdom more than anything else. Socrates took him to a nearby pond and repeatedly dunked the youth until all he could do was gasp for air. Then Socrates responded, "What is it you want?" The young man just stammered, "Air! I want Air!" Then Socrates finished, "When you yearn for wisdom like you yearn for air, you will get it without my help."

three examples of intimacy...

Isaiah: The Plan (Isaiah 6:1-8)	Jacob: The Process (Genesis 28-33)	Moses: The Price (Exodus 33:7-11) You Must Be Willing To:
1 Revelation of God (v.1-2)	1 Challenges & Choices Genesis 28	1 Separate Yourself Regularly (v.7)
2 Realization of His Holiness (v.3-4)	2 Divine Discipline Genesis 29-31	2 Seek After God with all Your Heart (v.7)
3 Recognition of Your Sinfulness (v.5)	3 Crisis & Collapse Genesis 32	3 Be Watched by the Public (v.8)
4 Renewal of Your Perspective (v.6-7)	4 Empowering & Enabling Genesis 32-33	4 Learn to listen and obey God's Voice (v.9)
5 Response of Your Lifestyle (v.8)		5 Enter Covenant Partnership with God (v.10-11)

Exodus 33.11

The Lord would speak to Moses face to face, as a man speaks to his friend.

(NLT)

reflect and respond

We can learn many things from these three men that will impact our own walk with God. What do you learn from these examples about your own intimacy with God?

assess yourself...

The last portion of this lesson is devoted to assessing your current intimacy with God. Relationships are difficult to assess because they are fluid and often change. But this is designed to help give you a feel for your intimacy with God. Answer the questions below to give you insight into your current intimacy with God.

Never Sometimes Often

☐ ☐ ☐ In your spare moments, do you find yourself thinking about Jesus, and His purpose in the world and for your life?

☐ ☐ ☐ Do you consider ways to please Him more than you do others or yourself?

☐ ☐ ☐ Do you look forward to taking time to spend with Him?

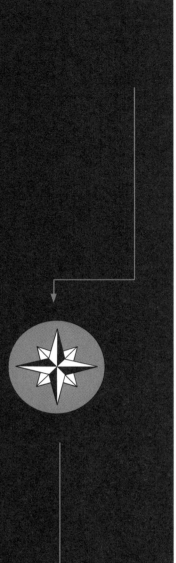

Never	Sometimes	Often	
☐	☐	☐	Can you describe Him "with your eyes closed?" (David didn't need to see Him physically to confidently describe His loving kindness, etc. We often hide behind the excuse that we need to see Him to feel close.)
☐	☐	☐	How well do you know His character from scripture? Can you point to specific times when you "proved" His character in your life?
☐	☐	☐	How frequently do you talk to others about Him?
☐	☐	☐	Is He your best friend?
☐	☐	☐	Do you hide certain things (topics) from Him as you pray about your life, and do you neglect certain areas as you pray? How frequently are you absolutely transparent about where you are?
☐	☐	☐	What kinds of subject matter do you talk to Him about? Do you go beyond rhetoric and facts, to intimate, honest feelings?
☐	☐	☐	Do you enjoy worshipping Him and look for new ways to express yourself to Him?
☐	☐	☐	Is your driving hunger to obey Him? Does this show in sacrificial surrender of your preferences to do His bidding?
☐	☐	☐	When you practice a Biblical command, is your motive love for Him, or keeping a checklist of do's and don'ts? Does loving God prompt your lifestyle?
☐	☐	☐	When you enter seasons of your life that are difficult and uncertain — do you trust Him?
☐	☐	☐	Do you live your life, primarily, from a spiritual posture of "brokenness" and gratitude?
☐	☐	☐	Do you believe you "hear His voice" (John 10)?
☐	☐	☐	When you think of God, does the thought first spark "fear" or dread — or, have you experienced Him as "Abba Father" and your thought is warm and inviting?

survey says...

Now, add your checkmarks. Every "often" represents a 3; every "sometimes" represents a 2; and every "never" represents a 1.

36-48: You're probably "very close" to God; intimacy has begun to grow!

22-35: You have a hunger, but need to mature; keep on growing!

10-21: You may be a bit distant; definitely focus yourself on getting to know Him.

real life...

I had a missionary friend who was frequently called away from home. It was tough on his family, but it was hardest for his little son. At the train station, the boy would cling to him as if to beg him not to go. Most of the time his dad would appease the boy by bringing him an apple (apples were a rare treat in this country). This would distract the child until after he was able to jump on the train and depart.

One day, when he knew the trip would be especially long, my friend brought two apples to the station. He knew it would be a tough departure. Sure enough, the little boy clamped onto his dad's hand with all of his might. Outside of the passenger car my friend was to board, he said, "Now son, I'm going to be home soon, I promise. But, just to make it better I brought you not one, but *two* apples."

He jammed them into his son's tiny hands and quickly hopped onto the train. After setting down his luggage, he glanced out the door to see if his son was still there. And he told me that as he looked out the opening of the train, he saw the child still standing in the same place he had left him. The apples had been dropped onto the concrete and he had tears rolling down his cheeks. He heard his little boy whimper, "But daddy, I don't want your apples . . . I want you."

bringing it all home...

I think God is looking for people that will say to Him, "Your answers to prayer are wonderful. But, even if I never got another answer, it would be enough to just know You." It's a pure state that I am talking about. No hidden agendas. Is this your heart's cry?

Look back at the plans you have made throughout this lesson. How are you going to wade into a deeper relationship with God? Commit to carrying out this plan and begin it right now!

how to do it...

Here are seven tips to building intimacy with God...

1. Spend extended time alone with God. Plot out maybe four times this year a day that you will spend a day alone with God. Take a notebook and Bible. You think it sounds boring? I've never been bored on a day alone with God.
2. Seek to please God. Regain that dating mindset with God.
3. Reflect on what God is doing in your life
4. Find a Christian who models intimacy. It is more caught than taught. Spend time with them and ask them questions about how they have gotten to the place that they are so tight with God.
5. Tell yourself the truth about your relationship with God.
6. Practice intimacy with your spouse and family. God gives us laboratories like the church and family because it is a chance to practice intimacy principles with people.
7. Participate in a forum that encourages intimacy with God.

security or sabotage?

how personal insecurity prevents effective leadership

During the term of President Ronald Reagan, leaders from seven industrial nations were meeting at the White House to discuss economic policy. Reagan has recounted that during the meeting he came across Canadian Prime Minister Pierre Trudeau who was strongly upbraiding British Prime Minister Margaret Thatcher. He was criticizing her, telling her that she was all wrong and that her policies wouldn't work. She stood there in front of him with her head up, listening until he was finished. Then she walked away.

Following the confrontation, Reagan went up to her and said, "Maggie, he should never have spoken to you like that. He was out of line, just entirely out of line. Why did you let him get away with that?"

Thatcher looked at Reagan and answered, "A woman must know when a man is simply being childish."

That story surely typifies Margaret Thatcher. It takes a strong, secure person to succeed as a world leader. And that is especially true when the person is a woman. As a world leader, Thatcher experienced much criticism. At one point, she was referred to as "the most unpopular woman in Britain." But she didn't waver under the criticism. She remained secure in her convictions and maintained her self-respect. She once said, "To me consensus seems to be the process of abandoning all beliefs, principles, values, and policies in search of something in which no one believes . . . What great cause would have been fought and won under the banner, 'I stand for consensus'?" Because of her security in both herself and her leadership, the "Iron Lady," as she was called, was elected to three consecutive terms as prime minister. She is the only British leader of the modern era ever to achieve that.

BASIC TRUTH

A leader's sense of emotional security will either stabilize or sabotage them more than anything else.

the facts of the matter...

Colleges and graduate schools cannot teach leaders to possess personal security and identity. Many of them fail to even address the topic, assuming those issues are already resolved in the hearts of the men and women who enter the program. But they are not. Struggles with insecurity are common among leaders in all different fields from politics to business to religion. Note the following statistics gathered from surveys among pastors.

- **70%** of pastors surveyed said their self-image is lower now than when they entered the ministry.
- **95%** of pastors say they don't have the leadership gifts to perform in the way their congregations expect them to perform.
- **75%** of pastors responded anonymously that they are intimidated by the lay leaders or staff with which they work.
- **65%** of pastors said they have seriously considered quitting the ministry within the last two months.

reflect and respond...

Why must leaders develop a strong sense of security?

to put it graphically...

Study the diagram below. Listed here are inner needs that each one of us have. If we assume a position of leadership without addressing these needs in healthy ways—we may experience a "train wreck" within our own personal lives...often in public. This is why personal security is essential to effective leadership.

inner need:	if missing, we feel:	common symptoms:
belonging	insecure	over-compensation, emotional highs and lows
worth	inferior	competition, self-doubt, need for recognition
competence	inadequate	comparison with specific people; defensive attitude
purpose	illegitimate	compulsive driven spirit, defeat, depression

reflect and respond...

Examine the inner needs and the common symptoms of each insecurity. At work, in school, or at home, which of these behaviors exhibit themselves in different pockets of your life? Reflect on the chart above and put a check by the symptoms you display. Now describe how you act out these symptoms in your behavior. (I cut others down; I try to "one up" my friends; I focus unduly upon myself in relationship and conversation, etc.)

spotting insecurity in your behavior...

We all have personal insecurities. When we approach new situations, it is normal to ask yourself, "Can I meet this new challenge?...I hope I have what it takes." But there is a kind of day-to-day insecurity in the life of many leaders. It prohibits them from seeing themselves correctly and therefore from seeing others around them correctly. Because of this insecurity, the leader's results, many times, are not what they would wish or are not what God would desire for them. To be honest, personal insecurity is fairly easy to spot in our behavior. We fail to see it merely because we ignore it. We pretend it isn't there by defending ourselves and diverting the focus on to something else. The following are six biblical case studies of ordinary people who struggled with different, common insecurities. Notice how it showed up in their lives.

46

six symptoms of insecurity...

I. COMPARISON:

We begin to compare ourselves to others and score ourselves against their achievements.

the parable of the vineyard workers

An example of this symptom occurs in Matthew 20 where Jesus speaks of the Parable of the Vineyard Workers. Take a minute to read this parable from Matthew 20 in your Bible. Then reflect on areas where you have exhibited attitudes of comparison to others.

Five truths about comparison spring out of this passage. Take a moment to honestly evaluated how you would act out personal security or insecurity if you were one of the vineyard workers that day. Those workers teach us that when you compare...

insecurity in your life

You ignore God's grace to you, being preoccupied with the status of others.

Never	Seldom	Occasionally	Often	Regularly

You grumble and complain about perceived inequities.

Never	Seldom	Occasionally	Often	Regularly

You judge others as less worthy of blessing than you.

Never	Seldom	Occasionally	Often	Regularly

You assume you deserve more because your focus is on your work not God's.

Never	Seldom	Occasionally	Often	Regularly

You forget that ALL reward and blessing is due to the grace of God.

Never	Seldom	Occasionally	Often	Regularly

reflect and respond...

Examine the three insecure actions listed on the sidebar. Take a minute and briefly write about a situation in your life that caused you to experience one of these reactions. How did you feel...how did you respond...what made you respond this way?

---

danger of comparison: we ignore the unique role that each of us plays on the team.

Three insecure actions

• I can't rejoice with those who succeed

• I get defensive about my own accomplishments

• I project my self-worth to others

God's perspective on this symptom: John 21.21-22

"When Peter noticed him, he asked Jesus, 'Master, what's going to happen to *him*?' Jesus said, 'If I want him to live until I come again, what's that to you? You—follow me .'"

(THE MESSAGE)

2. COMPENSATION:

We feel like victims and must now compensate for our losses or inferiority.

danger of compensation:
We fail to trust God's control by taking matters into our own hands, and by forcing issues. We over-compensate for where we feel we're weak.

God's perspective on this symptom:
Galatians 6.4-5
"Make a careful exploration of who you are and the work you have been given, and then sink yourself into that. Don't be impressed with yourself. Don't compare yourself with others. Each of you must take responsibility for doing the creative best you can with your own life."

(THE MESSAGE)

The second symptom of insecurity, compensation, is very familiar to us in today's society. People often fall into the grips of materialism in an effort to compensate for a weakness in their life. Sometimes men use expensive cars or lavish houses to make up for a perceived inferiority. Women can become obsessive about their appearance to compensate for some other deficiency—even to the point of developing an eating disorder. Leaders will do odd things to compensate for or cover up their deficiencies

jacob's life...

Insecurity is not a new idea—it has been around since the beginning of time. The Old Testament patriarch Jacob experienced it. As you read, inspect Jacob's life and see what you can learn about your own insecurities.

Read Genesis 27 and 32 about Jacob's life. See if you can pick up some of his insecurities, especially as they pertain to compensation. What words would you use to describe his behavior?

reflect and respond...

If, at the end of Jacob's life, we were able to listen to his thoughts as he reflected upon this early stage of his life, we might hear him making these five observations about compensation. See if any of them might be true of you at your present stage of life...

- We scheme how to get ahead and how to gain recognition.
- We begin to depend on personal politics to advance ourselves.
- We fail to recognize God's blessing on us because of our pursuit for more.
- We fight irrational battles to get what we think we deserve.
- We may stoop to dishonesty and deception to get results.

When have you demonstrated any of these actions in your life and leadership? Take a moment and write out a brief prayer asking God to forgive you for specific times when these actions characterized how you felt or how you acted.

3. COMPETITION:

We drift into self-centered patterns, consumed by outdoing others to receive attention and rewards.

A third symptom of insecurity is competition. When we honestly examine the motivation for the decisions that we make in leadership, too often we find that these decisions were motivated by competition. The competition might come from someone who is positioned under us and who we believe we must suppress, or it might come from a friend or a peer who we believe we must surpass.

healthy vs. harmful competition...

Now, just to clarify, there is both healthy competition and harmful competition. Healthy competition challenges both you and your competitor, sharpens both your skills, and results in a win-win situation. Michael Jordan would never have achieved his greatness without an extremely competitive spirit. I was reading a Sports Illustrated article detailing Michael's personal life, and it relayed how he competes in everything that he does. There is nothing he enjoys more in his free time than competing at ping-pong, pool, or another sport in his vast recreation room. He is extremely competitive, but his competitive fire is not fueled by insecurity. Harmful competition, by contrast, is rooted in insecurity. It is driven by the feelings that we must be first and others must be below us. It strives for a win-lose outcome where I must be at the center, or be the best, or get rewarded the most. When it comes to having a harmful competitive spirit, the older brother of the prodigal son would have given anyone a run for their money.

the "older" prodigal son...

Read Luke 15, the story of the prodigal son. Toward the end, (v. 28-30) try to spot some of the older brother's competitive words and actions. What are some similarities you see in both sons?

reflect and respond...

For the next biblical case studies we will drop in on an imaginary conversation between the biblical character and his or her counselor. We will get to hear the personal struggles with insecurity that each person experienced. The older prodigal son's therapist would probably have pointed out these negative competitive tendencies that the son was demonstrating. See if they sound familiar to you...

- You tend to keep score on life.
- You tend to be ungrateful.
- You tend to be unteachable.
- You tend to get jealous for recognition.
- You tend to be prideful.
- You tend to be critical and judgmental.
- You tend to be loveless.
- You tend to live a self-centered life.

49

danger of competition: we become obsessed with building our own kingdom, and eventually embrace the attitude that "the end will justify the means." We will do anything to win.

God's perspective on this symptom: Psalm 37.1-8

"Do not fret...do not be envious...trust in the Lord and do good. Dwell in the land and cultivate faithfulness. Delight yourself in the Lord and He will give you the desires of your heart. Commit your way to the Lord, trust also in Him and He will do it. Rest in the Lord...Do not fret... cease from anger ."

(NIV)

4. COMPULSION:

You are driven to perform compulsively to gain others' approval; you are a people-pleaser.

Ironically, in a society where we cherish our personal freedom to make decisions, the fourth symptom of insecurity, compulsion, strips away much of that freedom. It is easy to fall into the people-pleaser trap and to try to find our identity in what others think of us rather than what God thinks of us. There is no better example of this than Martha, who we read about in the New Testament.

martha's life...

Read Luke 10.38-42, the story of Martha's dinner party for Jesus. Notice how her activity was motivated by her compulsive spirit, not by love for her Savior. Why do you think that Jesus was not impressed by her "performance"?

reflect and respond...

Let's looks again at the imaginary conversation Martha had with her counselor about her compulsive tendencies. The counselor would have helped her realize that...

- She became distracted from "big picture" priorities, being consumed by her own performance.
- She projected her self-worth to others and over-estimated her importance.
- She experienced self-pity and sought recognition for her hard work.
- She grew weary because she attempted to do too much—for the wrong reasons.
- She tended to be a perfectionist.

You might recognize some of these characteristics if you have a propensity for slipping into a compulsive mindset. If you have found yourself in this mindset, ask God to help you overcome this insecurity. What people, situations, past experiences, or feelings cause you to fall into this performance trap?

50

5. CONDEMNATION:

The judgmental attitude of yourself or others, resulting in self-pity or self-conceit.

elijah's life...

Another type of symptom we may experience is condemnation. This type of insecurity manifests itself most often in our attitude. The prophet Elijah demonstrated this attitude during a difficult season in his ministry. Read I Kings 19, the story of Elijah fleeing after his encounter with the prophets of Baal. Join Elijah as he hosts a pity party, with himself as the star attraction. Then, interact to see if you've ever thrown a pity party like his.

As you read, think about how you suppose Elijah could plunge from a total victory in I Kings 18 to total despair in I Kings 19?

reflect and respond...

If, while we were finishing up sitting in on the counseling session with Martha, Elijah walked into the room and began to honestly share his feelings about his attitude, he might confess something like this...

- I have shortsighted perception of my circumstances.
- I feel self-pity and loneliness, as though I'm the only one to endure hardship.
- I complain about unjust circumstances and feel overwhelmed.
- I fear my demise and insignificance.
- I either project neurosis or a character disorder, blaming myself or others for everything wrong.

If you recognize some of these attitudes and action, meditate on Philippians 4:8-9 below:

Summing it all up, friends, I'd say you'll do best by filling your minds and meditating on things true, noble, reputable, authentic, compelling, gracious—the best, not the worst; the beautiful, not ugly; things to praise, not things to curse. Put into practice what you learned from me, what you heard and saw and realized. Do that, and God, who makes everything work together, will work you into his most excellent harmonies.

danger of condemnation
our distortion of reality and our being tempted to withdraw from responsibility.

God's perspective on this symptom:
1 Corinthians 4.3-5
"It matters very little to me what you think of me, even less where I rank in popular opinion. I don't even rank myself. Comparison in these matters are pointless. .. The *Master* makes that judgment. So don't get ahead of the Master and jump to conclusions with your judgments before all the evidence is in. When He comes, He will bring out in the open and place in evidence all kinds of things we never even dreamed of—inner motives and purposes and prayers. Only then will any one of us get to hear the 'Well done!' of God."

(THE MESSAGE)

6. CONTROL:

In order to validate your own worth, you feel as though you must take charge, protect your own interests and monopolize situations.

sarah's life...

The sixth symptom of insecurity that can cripple our leadership is the need for control. Our need for control is often evidenced by our trying to run a another person's agenda or by our manipulating relationships to get what we want from them. In the Old Testament, Sarah's life was permeated by a need for control. When she became uncertain of God's promise, she took control of the situation and tried to bring about God's will by her own means. Read Genesis 16:1-6 and look and see if your behavior ever resembles Sarah's. What thoughts, words, or actions do you identify with as she attempts to control her situation?

reflect and respond...

If Sarah would have stepped back from her dilemma and evaluated her feelings and actions, she might have seen her controlling behavior. If she did, she would have seen that...

- She felt God was inattentive, absent or even against her.
- Her circumstances determined her understanding of God's character.
- She viewed life as scarce rather than abundant.
- She became self-seeking and manipulative of others.
- She felt intimidated and she dealt with others through intimidation.
- She resented the success of others and even turned on them in anger.
- She felt if someone succeeds, then someone else must lose.
- She frequently blamed others for her dilemma.

rewind <<<

We all have insecurities, and, as we honestly realize them, we can work and pray to strengthen these areas. Reflect back upon your life to this point...which of these six insecurities best characterize the negative habits that you have fallen into? List the insecurities below (Comparison, Compensation, Competition, Compulsion, Condemnation, Control). Then, stop and pray for yourself and others who work with you. Write your prayer below . . .

 HALF TIME... continue the chapter next meeting

52

rewind <<<

We just examined the six symptoms of insecurity and are ready to take great strides in our development of personal security. To refresh your memory, look back at the six symptoms and remember which ones you most identified with. And now, let's look at what to do when insecurity raises its ugly head.

WHEN INSECURITY RAISES ITS UGLY HEAD . . .

Often, as leaders, our struggle with personal security comes and goes. We feel as if we've won the war during times of success or popularity among the people we lead. However, insecurity raises its ugly head most often when things aren't going well. Below are several circumstances that tend to reveal insecurity.

eight insecurity-building scenarios...

1. **CRITICISM AND REJECTION**

   When colleagues or subordinates attack our performance or character.

2. **MEETING SOMEONE IMPORTANT**

   When we're first introduced to someone we feel we must impress.

3. **FAILURE AT AN ASSIGNMENT**

   When we fail to reach a goal or standard, and we take it personally.

4. **A COLLEAGUE'S SUCCESS**

   When a peer achieves notoriety and reward for their own success.

5. **UNRECOGNIZED ACHIEVEMENT**

   When people we respect fail to notice our success and accomplishment.

6. **PERSONAL LOSS**

   When people and resources we've relied upon are taken away.

7. **REFLECTING ON AN UNFAIR PAST**

   When we become melancholy about our own victimized, unjust background.

8. **UNFAMILIAR TERRITORY**

   When we find ourselves in a new and unfamiliar situation.

reflect and respond...

When has one of these scenarios sparked feelings of insecurity in your life? Describe the situation .

summary:
six symptoms
of insecurity ...

comparison
compensation
competition
compulsion
condemnation
control

When I first became a pastor, at age 19, I met a colleague who struggled with insecurity. He told me that the board of elders at his church intimidated him. Then, he told me the church congregation intimidated him. I listened for an hour to the stories he told about his low self-esteem. He constantly lived with intimidation and anxiety. He was always second guessing himself.

That conversation shed light on the events at his church over the next four years. The church almost split. Board meetings were cruel and angry. In fact, the church would have split had they not fired my friend from his position.

What's sad about this story is this. It wasn't that he was a bad pastor or had poor people skills or theology. It was simply a story of a leader with emotional deficiencies who sabotaged his leadership.

THE LIES WE BELIEVE...

It is possible to waffle between the six symptoms, and even experience several at the same time. The key to successfully handling insecurity is to identify how we cope with our insecurity, and what kind of lies we tell ourselves about the reality we face.

Consider this: If the truth makes us free *(John 8.32)*, then lies put us in bondage. The level of defeat and bondage we face as leaders may be directly linked to the volume of myths or lies we've embraced about our identity. Our problem is that while we *know* the truth....we often *believe* the lie. Dr. Chris Thurman has written an insightful book entitled, *The Lies We Believe*. He provides a helpful process for us to understand.

How to step into the truth...

Determine — the trigger event that fostered the lie/bondage.
These steps are integral to freeing you from wrong thinking. What is an event that triggered insecurity within you? Write it below:

Discover — the lie you've believed about that situation.
What lie have you believed in this situation?

Decide — what response is truthful, appropriate and realistic.
What is your truthful, appropriate, and realistic response to this event and lie?

truths to live by...

- Never put your emotional health in the hands of someone else.
- The truth is a requirement for spiritual and emotional health.
- Most of our unhappiness and insecurity is the result of lies we believe.
- Recognize that you will believe what you *want* to believe.
- The truth can be eclipsed by a thrilling lie.
- A secret to healthy living is negotiating and balancing life's hardships.
- Remember that hurting people naturally hurt people; intimidated people intimidate.
- We can only pass on what we possess, ourselves.

God's perspective: John 8.32

"Then you will experience for yourselves the truth, and the truth will free you."

(THE MESSAGE)

example:
Your supervisor failed to affirm the hard work you put in on last week's successful outreach event. You feel resentful and insignificant.

example:
Perhaps you've embraced the lie, "I am only as good as what I do." You've attached your value to performance, and the approval of others.

example:
My personal worth is tied to who I am not what I do. My supervisor does appreciate me, but is human like me and likely failed to notice my work due to an oversight. After all, he has been very busy himself.

4 KEYS TO PERSONAL SECURITY...

In the final pages of this lesson, we will examine four keys to personal security: Identity, Brokenness, Purpose, and Giving and Receiving "The Blessing." There is a diagram for each key, which should make it easier for us to gain a handle on the truth. Study each diagram and embrace the truth completely. This may be the beginning of a wonderful leadership journey...where we each can be prevented from sabotaging ourselves and our leadership due to personal insecurities.

key one: IDENTITY

You must tie your self-worth to your identity in Christ, not people or performance.

2 Corinthians 5.16-18 reveals three biblical truths that are often forgotten as we develop our identity:

- **I have a New Position: I am now placed "in Christ" as well as "in the world".** (v.17a)
- **I Have New Possessions: I have been given "things" or resources inside of me.** (v.17b-18a)
- **I Have New Potential: I have been given these to fulfill a ministry to others.** (v.18b)

Throughout the New Testament, God reveals to us our true identity in Christ. Look at this diagram we'll see later in section 6, "who do you think you are?" See "what's gotten into you!"

We need to do much more than simply acknowledge who we are in Christ—we need to act on it! Write a brief statement about what it means to you to know who you are in Christ. What past baggage do these truths release you from? What purpose does these truths constrain you to pursue?

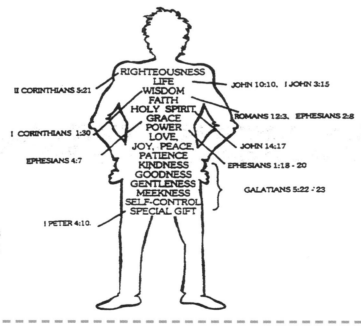

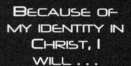

BECAUSE OF MY IDENTITY IN CHRIST, I WILL . . .

Renew My Perspective:
See myself based on my position, not my experience.

Release My Past:
Let go of old images, sins, and baggage that prevents growth.

Remember My Purpose:
Remind myself I've been left here to minister as a change agent.

God's perspective:
Genesis 32.24-28

"So Jacob was left alone, and a man wrestled with him till daybreak. When the man saw that he could not overpower him, he touched the socket of Jacob's hip so that his hip was wrenched as he wrestled with the man. Then the man said, 'Let me go for it is daybreak.' But Jacob replied, 'I will not let you go unless you bless me.'
The man asked him, 'What is your name?' 'Jacob,' he answered.
Then the man said, 'Your name will no longer be Jacob, but Israel, because you have struggled with God and with men and have overcome...'"

(NIV)

Fact

what I view as my source will determine my course.

key two: BROKENNESS

You must allow God to break you of self-sufficiency and self-promotion.

The second key to developing security is brokenness. We all want the grace and blessing of God on our lives. But, God "gives grace to the humble." Brokenness is the pathway to experience what we really want and need. If I am not broken by God, I will continue to resolve my insecurities with my own strength and old patterns. Jacob wrestled with God for twenty years, before finally learning the essentials of His grace & blessing. These essentials are also what we need:

four biblical essentials for brokenness...

He was ALONE with God:	He was HONEST to God:	He was HUNGRY for God:	He was BROKEN by God:
He could lean on nothing else; he had no other source.	He stopped lying about his identity; he confessed who he was	He determined he wouldn't leave until God blessed him.	He was broken of his stubborn, self-sufficient lifestyle.

Often, our insecurity can lead us into a vicious cycle. The only One who can stop the cycle is God. When we hit rock-bottom in our lives, we must be broken before Him.

david's life...

King David, when he was ruler of Israel, also longed to experience the grace and blessing of God in his leadership after his selfish sin with Bathsheba. Read Psalm 51 and notice the sequence of his brokenness before God in prayer...

1. His plea for cleansing (v. 1-3)
2. His recognition of the barrier He had created (v. 4)
3. His acknowledgement of the truth (v. 5-9)
4. His hunger for God's presence (v. 10-13)
5. His worshipping posture (v. 14-15)
6. His broken and contrite heart (v. 16-17)

Brokenness before God is essential to our spiritual health and leadership. Right now, quiet your heart before God...Ask him if there is sin in your life...If so, begin these same biblical steps that David took. When you are finished, write down what God has spoken to your heart:

key three: PURPOSE

You must discover and practice your God-given purpose in life, not someone else's.

The third key to our security is purpose. Just as Jesus was sent with a specific mission to accomplish, so we are sent to accomplish a specific purpose with each of our lives. We are to link our lives with God's purposes for the world.

fit the pieces together...

God made your life to be a beautiful puzzle. He wove together all of your different gifts, desires, and experiences into the unique picture of you. He did this so that you would be able to accomplish his purpose and plan for your life. Underneath each heading, write where you fit into God's plan...

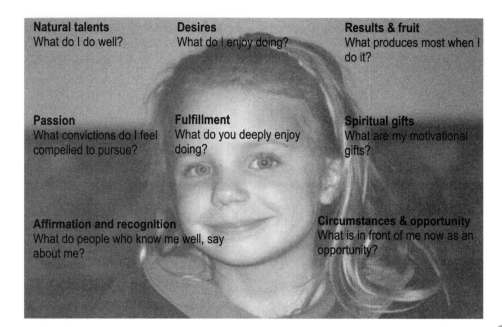

Natural talents
What do I do well?

Desires
What do I enjoy doing?

Results & fruit
What produces most when I do it?

Passion
What convictions do I feel compelled to pursue?

Fulfillment
What do you deeply enjoy doing?

Spiritual gifts
What are my motivational gifts?

Affirmation and recognition
What do people who know me well, say about me?

Circumstances & opportunity
What is in front of me now as an opportunity?

Your life mission ought to . . .

- Start with yourself
- Contain life-changing convictions
- Include others
- Be bigger than yourself
- Have eternal values
- Center on God's priorities to reach the world

reflect and respond...

In several sentences, attempt to write out what you believe is the mission God has given you.

God's perspective: John 17.4

"...Jesus said... 'I have brought You glory on earth by completing the work You gave me to do.'"

(NIV)

1 Corinthians 15.10

"But by the grace of God I am what I am, and His grace to me was not without effect. No, I worked harder than all them — yet not I, but the grace of God that was with me."

(NIV)

your life mission . . .

Developing a life mission statement can be a major undertaking. But there is no better time to begin than now! If you have not already developed a personal life mission statement, commit to beginning the process over the next several months.

God's perspective:
Genesis 27.21, 28-29

"Then Isaac said to Jacob, 'Come over here. I want to touch you . . . May God always bless and give you plenty of dew for healthy crops and good harvest of grain and wine. May many nations become your servants. May you be the master of your brothers. May all your mother's sons bow low before you. All who curse you are cursed, and all who bless you are blessed.'"

(NLT)

key four: GIVING AND RECEIVING "THE BLESSING"

You must learn to let others love and bless you, and to do the same for them.

a father's blessing...

The fourth and final key to developing personal security is giving and receiving "the blessing." In the Old and New Testaments, fathers would "bless" their sons. This was more than just a simple prayer for them. It was a display of affection, it was a passing of authority and an expression of faith in that son. In one sense, it was a rite of passage into manhood.

The story of Jacob and Esau reminds us that "the blessing" was something cherished by boys; it was not uncommon for them to struggle for the blessing that dad would deliver. While we don't have a name for it today—people still fight over receiving the blessing from authority figures and those they respect. According to John Trent and Gary Smalley, the "blessing" was an expression of love, and consisted of five ingredients:

the blessing...

- **SPOKEN WORD** — We need to be affirmed by others.
- **MEANINGFUL TOUCH** — We need to be embraced and touched by others.
- **EXPRESSION OF HIGH VALUE** — We need to have our strengths recognized.
- **VISION OF A SPECIAL FUTURE** — We need someone to believe in our future.
- **APPLICATION OF GENUINE COMMITMENT** — We need someone to see us through the process.

reflect and respond...

Make a list of people who you need to give "the blessing" to. What can you do to give them "the blessing?" Now, TODAY, bless these people and add value to their lives. Write out their names and a make commitment to do this now!

he root of the problem...

When we get beyond the surface, we see that at the root of our struggle, is the issue self-worth. Items above it are symptomatic of this deeper issue. In our behavior, we spot negative patterns. Just below the surface, we can identify negative attitudes or emotions. we dig deeper, we most often see the issue of unforgiveness, and deeper than that issue is the ue of unmet needs. We expect someone to meet a need, and when they fail, we cannot forgive m. However, if you dig down to the very root of the problem, you see the real issue is self-worth. s is why the body of Christ must commit to receive and give the "blessing" to each other.

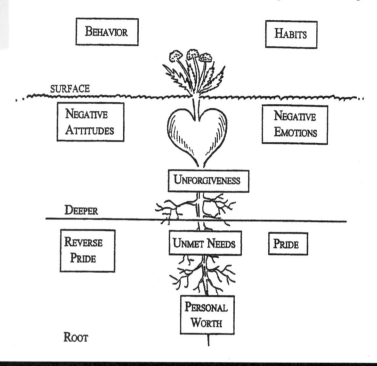

God's perspective
1 John 4:18-21

"There is no room in love for fear. Well-formed love banishes fear. Since fear is crippling, a fearful life—fear of death, fear of judgment—is one not yet fully formed in love. We, though, are going to love—love and be loved. First we were loved, now we love. He loved us first.

"If anyone boasts, 'I love God,' and goes right on hating his brother or sister, thinking nothing of it, he is a liar. If he won't love the person he can see, how can he love the God he can't see? The command we have from Christ is blunt: Loving God includes loving people. You've got to love both."

(THE MESSAGE)

assess yourself...

Reflect back on the lesson as a whole and evaluate how secure you are as a person and as a leader. When a follower has a great idea, do you suppress it or support it? Do you celebrate your people's victories, or do you try to "one-up" them because you're the leader? When your team succeeds, do you give the members the credit? Rate yourself on a scale of 1 to 10. Where are you and why?

How often do you experience definite feelings of insecurity in your life and leadership? Each day, each week, each year?

From what you have learned about leadership so far, would you consider your personal security to be a strength or weakness in your life and leadership? Why?

Fact

You can't lead people if you need people.

what I can do to develop security...

- Study and meditate on the scriptures that define your identity in Christ. What Scriptures will I meditate on?

  ____

- Check yourself each time you compare yourself to someone. Pause and thank God for the differences that He has given you.
- Focus your attention on your strengths for a season. Identify and polish your gifts and skills. What are my strengths?

  ____

  What will I do to develop them?

  ____

  ____

- Read and listen to motivational material: books, tapes, magazines, etc. What books, tapes, or magazines will I invest in?

  ____

- Identify the two or three most common lies you believe about yourself. Write down the truth about those areas, then tell yourself the truth.

  ____

  ____

- Find someone who is "safe" to be a support person. Practice giving and receiving the love, encouragement, and truth you both need. Who is that person?

  ____

- Remind yourself of the truth: we are to imitate Christ—who came and emptied himself in order to serve others, not be served.

bringing it all home...

French novelist Honoré de Balzac was a keen observer of human nature, and he sought to capture a complete picture of modern civilization in his huge work *The Human Comedy*. He once observed, "Nothing is a greater impediment to being on good terms with others than being ill at ease with yourself." Don't let insecurity prevent you from reaching your potential!

becoming a person of
INFLUENCE

how God builds a person into a leader

It was 1921 when Dr. Evan Kane first proposed the idea of doing surgery on someone using only local anesthesia. Up until then, doctors had always put patients to sleep, knocking them out for hours afterward. He wanted to do it with the patient wide awake. His New York hospital approved of it, but only if he could find his own patient. He went to work on finding a patient and date to perform this historic surgery. On February 15, it all happened. Meticulously, he removed the appendix from the patient. When he sowed the skin back up, it was such a success that all on-lookers broke out into applause. It was one for the record books. Here's the irony. The surgeon that day in 1921, was Dr. Evan Kane, and the patient...was also Dr. Evan Kane. That day he did surgery on himself!

As we grow into spiritual leaders, some inward surgery will have to be done. I believe that no one can do it for us. We must choose to take out those things that hinder our growth and cooperate with God's pruning process. This story illustrates precisely what I want to accomplish here. This chapter will provide you with the scalpel and the scissors for you to do the necessary surgery on your life and leadership.

the BIG picture

There's one more analogy I want to provide that will illustrate what I want to accomplish. An eight-year old boy was trying to watch a parade by peering through a knothole in a fence. He could only see whatever came along directly in front of him: first a clown, then the band, next came a float. At one point, his dad came behind him and hoisted him high above the fence. For the first time, he could see the panorama of the *entire* parade!

That is the purpose of this lesson. It is designed to lift us up above our lives and to give us an overview of the journey of maturity God desires to take us on throughout our lifetimes. We will examine **God's objectives** in each phase of our development as well as our **appropriate responses** to those phases. Why is this important for us to understand? Because if we can see the big picture of what God is trying to accomplish, we can begin to cooperate with God in the surgical process. Let's fasten our seatbelts . . . we're about to see the big picture of the incredible adventure awaiting us!

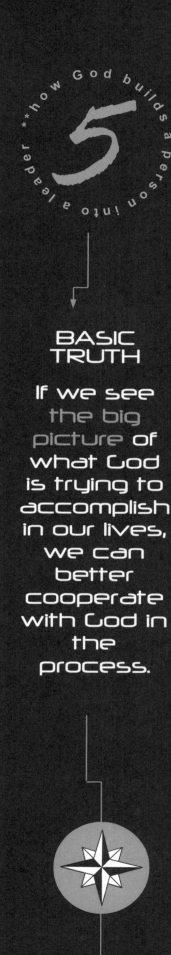

5

BASIC TRUTH

If we see the big picture of what God is trying to accomplish in our lives, we can better cooperate with God in the process.

one bite at a time...

We all wish maturity would come instantly—but that's not realistic. Before we look at the phases, let's look at some passages that illustrate the idea of *progressive* growth:

Read 1 John 2.12-14. In this text, John speaks to three different groups of people, who represent three stages of spiritual maturity. Notice that each group (fathers, young men, and children) all face different issues in their life. What does this passage teach you about God's view of growth?

Also read:
- Matthew 25.21
- Jeremiah 12.5
- 1 Peter 2.2
- Hebrews 5.12-6.3
- Colossians 2.6-7
- 1 Corinthians 3.1-3

our six phases...

Growth comes in many different forms and often it does not happen as we expect it to. But, we can recognize certain landmarks along the way. This lesson will put our lives in the form of six phases—from birth to death—but the rate at which we go through these phases will differ for each individual. As we work through these phases, think about where you have been, where you are, and where you want to be. It's time to look over the fence and see the big picture!

Phase One: providential beginnings

This stage generally covers our lives from birth up to conversion. It includes all the things that happen before we get together with God. Isn't it great to know that He uses us even in the times of life before we are cooperating with Him? He is completely providential and sovereign. He is already preparing us to be used by him.

God's objectives for phase one...

personality development
God desires our unique development (temperament, talents, preferences, style, character).

testimony development
God is building a story of His grace. He uses everything—the good and the bad.

teachability

We must each recognize the need for His control. Our world today sends messages demanding that we be "in control" at all times. It usually takes deliberate thought and action to surrender ourselves to His control.

basic ethics

God wants to build in us an awareness of right and wrong. We begin to think like He thinks.

healthy attitude and emotions

God desires to construct a foundation of positive attitudes and emotional health. This perspective will be optimal for what He wants to do later.

the construction of a life...

Your life can be compared to the building of a house. Phase One is like the foundation of the house. The concrete slab that every home is built upon may appear boring prior to the walls being constructed. Have you ever driven through a new neighborhood when all you could see was a cement foundation and a few pipes sticking up from the ground? Definitely boring. However, that foundation is most critical, and paramount to the endurance of the structure. Get the point? The same is true with our lives. Phase One may seem uneventful and unglamorous—but it's the foundation upon which the rest of your life is built!

reflect and respond...

Go through each of these objectives. Identify ways God has developed them in your life. What is unique about you? What attributes exist inside you that make you different.

your part...

- Have a positive attitude and perspective toward all circumstances, realizing that God is preparing you for something.
- Take advantage of the lessons God teaches at this foundational stage!

Shortcuts
don't pay
off in the
long run!

Neglecting
personal
disciplines
makes us like
houses with
termites . . .
We look great
on the
outside, but
we are
crumbling on
the inside.

Phase Two: character & spiritual formation

Once we pass through Providential Beginnings, Phase Two begins. It optimally begins at our conversion. For the first time, we can choose to cooperate with God's purposes for us. His purpose is to develop our spirit and our character. His focus is on our private, personal disciplines, not so much the development of our talents or skills. We tend to by-pass these character builders because they bring us no immediate fan-fare or glamour; no spotlights or microphones. Motivation can be tough because it often must come from within. Few people at work evaluate our quiet time with God and we will never be promoted based on our scripture memory or intimacy with God. Most people (even leaders) find it difficult to consistently focus on these disciplines.

Our temptation is to take short cuts on our character development. We want to hurry through this stage of our life. We yearn to move on to outward skills and charisma; the things that others see and applaud. After all, what's the big deal about our character?

real life...

A millionaire contracted a builder to construct a house for him. The budget was $400,000 and the builder was told to keep any money left over from the project. Because he wanted to make as much money for himself as he could, the builder scrimped on everything possible in every part of the house. Taking many short cuts, he built the house as fast as he could. When he finally got done, he went back to the millionaire and said, "The house is done, **here are the keys!**" The millionaire grabbed the keys, smiled and pushed them back into the man's hands and stated, "The house, dear sir, is yours."

The builder had the chance to create a mansion for himself, yet he chose to build a flimsy shack, not knowing he was cheating himself. Overlooking our character development results in a similar surprise. God hands over our lives to us and lets us do with it as we like. When we cut corners on the important basics, we are like the builder. We think we are getting away with something when we do just enough to be a good person, but ignore the solid formation of our spirit and character.

God's objectives for phase two...

intimacy
God desires a close relational experience with us, not just a cognitive, academic understanding of Him. Read John 15.9 and John 17.3.

discernment
God wants us to develop the ability to distinguish between right and wrong. We begin to think like God thinks, and value what He values. Read I Corinthians 2.14-16.

lordship

God desires us to obey out of love for Him, not out of duty or performance. This is settling the Lordship issue: He calls the shots, we don't. Read Matthew 7.21, Luke 6.46

security

God desires us to develop a deep inner life. This means our security is cemented in the truth of Scripture, not in the lies of society. If we start serving without a sense of personal security, we will eventually sabotage ourselves. Read Galatians 6.3-5.

identity

God desires us to possess a healthy self-image and self-esteem where our identity is established in who He says we are. Identity and security are virtually inseparable. If we don't get our identity settled, the pressures of leadership will surely shape us into someone we never intended to become. Read II Corinthians 5.16-18.

convictions and disciplines

Another objective God has for us in this stage is the development of personal convictions and spiritual disciplines. These enable us to delay gratification and live on purpose. They also strengthen the infrastructure of our lives so we can stand when the heat is on. God knows how foundational these objectives are to the health and vitality of our lives. Without them in place, we would not make it very far without problems!

reflect and respond...

Review God's objectives in this phase. Which areas are the strongest in your life right now? Which areas are weakest in your life right now?

What disciplines do you need to build into your life right now?

"Being" must come before "doing," because if you are somebody, you will naturally do something.

WHAT I AM	WHAT I DO	RESULT
Humble	Rely on God	Power
People Lover	Give	Security
Visionary	Set Goals	High Morals

This diagram was developed by Dr. John Maxwell. In it he illustrates the need to move from the left column (what I am) toward the right column (result) via the middle column (what I do). But, because we are so preoccupied with results, performance, and production, we're often tempted to move from right to left. We need to focus on "being" before "doing," if we are ever going to achieve permanent results

For instance, we may be so consumed with desiring to see power in our lives (result column), that we move leftward and try feverishly to rely on God since that's what produces a powerful life. Most of the time our attempts are done in our own strength and are short-lived. We become frustrated.

God is saying to us, however, "Why don't you simply *become* humble? Why not develop humility in your 'being'—then you will naturally rely on me, and the result will be power." Jesus taught that a good tree naturally bears good fruit.

reflect and respond...

Do you see patterns of "doing" before "being" in your own life? What things can you do to reverse your focus?

Why is it difficult for you to address these Phase Two issues?

your part...

- Become involved in some form of ministry or service. Spiritual muscles are exercised by serving!
- Be faithful and consistent in your personal disciplines.
- Meditate regularly in the Word. Know it and derive your self-image from it.
- Ask God to break you and shape you.

Phase Three: service & application

By Phase Three, it's time to leave the bench and start working! In the early stages of our Christian life, most of our growth comes from listening to instruction. By this phase, God draws a line in the sand and states, "You've got to get up and do something about what you know, or you will stunt your growth." In Phase Three, the primary means of growth is action. It comes from applying what you know. Now you're prepared to balance nutrition (milk) with exercise (meat).

how we grow and mature...

Read Hebrews 5.12-6.3. The text talks about two kinds of Christians: babies and mature adults. It speaks of two kinds of food: milk and meat (solid food).
Notice that the items we would list under the "milk" category are primarily instructional in nature, (6.1-2). The items we would list under the "meat" category are application in nature, (5.14).
In other words, contrary to modern belief, "meat" is not simply deeper teaching or preaching on Sunday morning. It is obedience. It is practicing the "milk."   Even Jesus said, "My meat is to DO the will of Him who sent me" (John 4.34).

BABIES	MATURE
"milk"	"meat"
Instruction (Hebrews 6.1-2)	Application (Hebrews 5.14)

reflect and respond...

What does this say to us about God's view of maturity?

What does it say about Phase Three in our leadership growth?

God's objectives for phase three...

submission

God desires our submission and our loyalty to authority . . . even when we disagree with them. We won't be good leaders unless we first learn to be good followers. If we don't learn to listen and submit now, how will we do it when we are the leader?

vision/purpose

God desires to develop in us a burden and a vision, in that order. Our life purpose is often revealed as we develop these, and experiment with different types of ministry. When we begin to see where our passions lie, our purpose becomes much clearer.

people skills/shepherd's heart

God desires that we become a lover of people and that we develop people skills and discernment in relationships. Even before we master techniques for ministry—we are to develop a deep compassion for others that moves us into action.

real life...

Hoping to share his faith in Christ, a friend of mine, named Eric, gave a tract to a man on the street. He had no idea this man was an atheist. The man's anger toward God became evident as he ripped up the tract and hissed profanity at Eric. Ironically, instead of retaliating in defense, tears welled up in Eric's eyes. He didn't say a word. He just stood there on the sidewalk, crying. When the atheist looked up and finally saw his tears, he was stunned. After an awkward pause, the atheist quietly stooped down to pick up his litter, stuffed the ripped pages in his pocket and walked away.

A few days later Eric's phone rang. It was the stranger he had met on the street. The man explained that after taping the tract back together, he discovered my friend's number on the back . . . and wanted to let him know that he had read it through twice and prayed "that little prayer" at the end to invite Christ to take over his life. He'd been transformed.

Eric was dumbfounded. He didn't know what to say except, "Why?" The atheist answered, "I've never seen anyone truly care about whether I got it or not. I thought Christians were just angry and narrow people going through the motions. But, for the first time, I saw someone who really cared about me—and I figured I ought to read what you had to say."

the bottom line...

It was a **shepherd's heart**, not eloquence that was needed in this situation. It took a vessel of genuine character and compassion to get the truth through to the unbeliever standing in front of him. God refines our hearts, getting the **inner qualities** in place so that we are able to do the same.

identification of motivational gift

Optimally, in this phase, we locate our spiritual gift-mix, and begin to identify our primary motivational gift (Romans 12). This gift is the central "hub", around which our other gifts will revolve. We begin to understand who we are and who we are not; our strengths and weaknesses.

responsibility

Here we must recognize that to make things happen, we are responsible to initiate action. We cannot sit around waiting for a wise mentor or a perfect service opportunity to come our way. We've got to assume responsibility for our lives and go after what we know will help us grow.

sacrifice

We must become willing to give up rights and relationships in order to grow. In order to get us where God wants to us to go, He teaches us that we must surrender the things that may be hindering our growth. This may mean giving up a dating relationship or a friendship, or a habit that we have. At this point, we surrender our lives to a "giving mode" rather than a "receiving mode."

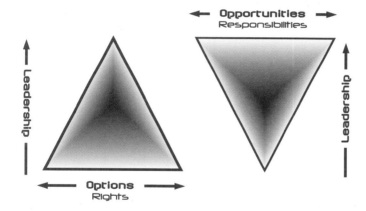

As we move up in leadership, the amount of responsibility and sacrifice in our life must increase. When first coming to Christ (the base of the triangle) we have the widest amount of options – we may possess some bad habits, but praise God, He still lets us into the Kingdom. But as we move upward into ministry and leadership, those options narrow. Unlike the world around us, leadership means giving up options, not gaining them (Matthew 20.25). Our goal is to reach the pinnacle of that triangle where we can declare with the apostle Paul, "I am a bond-servant of Jesus Christ."

reflect and respond...

Can you spot something possibly hindering your growth right now? What is keeping you from giving it up?

your part...

- Become strictly accountable to a ministry position.
- Work to develop relationships.
- Experiment with your spiritual gift mix to understand your strengths and weaknesses.
- Become a strategic prayer warrior.
- Master time management – make a "time budget" to redeem the time instead of waste time.
- Share your faith regularly.
- Narrow your focus. Begin to zero in on your mission in life.

the construction of a life...

If we were to continue our "house" analogy, Phase Three represents all of the functional dimensions of the house: the plumbing, the electricity, the heating and air conditioning, and other items that make it work. It's now livable and functional.

reflect and respond...

Are you anywhere near this phase in your own life? How much "milk" and "meat" do you partake of in your life right now? Do you practice what you know?

rewind <<<

As we walk through the journey of life, different experiences will mark our development. Take a moment to review the first three phases. What phase are you in now? What experiences brought you through the previous phases?

Look especially at the section titled "God's Objectives" in Phases Two and three. Are you currently working through any of those objectives? Which ones? What do you need to do to continue growing in those areas?

 HALF TIME... continue the chapter next meeting

In this lesson, we are taking a big picture look at our lives and the growth that we are or are not experiencing. We've looked at the first three phases of life, let's review those again.

Phase One: Providential Beginnings
Phase Two: Character and Spiritual Formation
Phase Three: Service and Application

Now we will take a look at the remaining three phases . . .

Phase Four:
momentum & reproduction

In this phase, God expects spiritual fruit to be produced from our lives. Phase Four usually begins in mid-life, where we are no longer a mere student in God's economy. He now sees us as a "laborer" who ought to be bearing fruit for the Kingdom. This phase is a combination of phase two ("being") and three ("doing") merging together in our lives. This phase typically begins the most fruitful years of life.

Just as Joseph endured a long season of testing, and Moses endured a long season of obscurity—we, too, must ready ourselves for this phase, where our most productive years will occur. Often in this stage we begin to focus on our ultimate contribution in life.

God's objectives for phase four...

priorities
God desires us to have a definite grasp on priorities. We must be able to discern what is best and when to say "no" to things. We are no longer a slave to the "immediate" but are giving ourselves to the "ultimate."

fruitfulness
God desires us to become mature in our fruitfulness. This makes us effective as soul-winners and in areas of service. We know how to make it happen, and how to get the job done. We are productive and fruitful in some arena.

motives
God desires us to please Him more than people. Our motives for ministry must be correct! We do the right things for the right reasons.

motives . . .

We must be more concerned about pleasing God than we are about pleasing man.

spiritual reproduction

God desires us to be able to pass on transferable concepts to others under us. We are able to mentor and disciple others effectively and completely (Colossians 1.28-29). We master the issue of spiritual reproduction—and produce disciples who produce disciples.

communion as a lifestyle

God desires us to commune with Him on a regular basis, regardless of the hardships we face. We must be positive and teachable in our response to His life lessons.

real life ...

At the turn of the 20th century, two young boys struggled with polio. Both grew up in the same neighborhood, and were victims of an age that had no vaccine for the disease. As they entered adulthood, their attitudes began to polarize. One decided to give up on anything close to a normal life. He became a recluse and took a pessimistic perspective on life. Although he was the more gifted of the two, he eventually became bitter and fatalistic. The other resolved to make the most of his disease and see it as a way to identify with others enduring hardship. He made it all the way to the top. He was President Franklin D. Roosevelt.

the construction of a life...

As we continue our house analogy, Phase Four represents the work on the exterior of the house. The outward walls have all been put up, and everyone can see what the house has become—what it looks like. When built well, the house is not only beautiful to look at, but provides secure covering from the weather. The structure is fully functional for others to dwell in.

What is Phase Four about?

A Lifestyle of Surrender

All things are done for the Kingdom's sake and for the advancement of the gospel, not for the advancement of ourselves.

reflect and respond...

Describe what you hope your life will look like at Phase Four.

your part

- Begin to handle isolation, conflict and crisis with trust.
- Define your gift mix. Your role is clear in body of Christ.
- Develop effective communication skills.
- Delegate to others and control your ego!
- Think through and implement a Biblical strategy for ministry.
- Understand and apply the 80/20 principle – when your priorities are right, 20% of your time is yielding 80% of your results (with wrong priorities, it is possible that 80% of your time will yield 20% of your results).

Phase Five:
convergence & significance

The next stage is one of great fulfillment. Few leaders attain it. It all occurs when three factors converge together:

- The leader
- The task
- The context

In other words, who we are, the work we do and the people we do it with all come together. Our lives flourish because all these factors have come together. Consider Bill McCartney, who left his coaching career at the University of Colorado to give leadership full time to Promise Keepers. Consider Chuck Swindoll, who left the Evangelical Free Church in Fullerton, California to become president of Dallas Theological Seminary and to plant a church in Dallas. Consider John Maxwell, who left Skyline Wesleyan Church in San Diego, California in order to devote his time to training pastors to become more effective leaders. A match occurred as those men made those moves.

God's objectives for phase five...

effectiveness
God desires us to have a leadership/ministry match that provides maximum, visible effectiveness. God will continue to test us because He is looking for deep effectiveness in our lives. His tests help us to zero in on the central legacy we are to leave.

wisdom/objectivity
God desires us to apply relevant knowledge to life. The more people we have influence over, the more cautiously we must make decisions in ministry. Our life experience has taught us which battles are worth fighting and which are not.

world vision
God desires us to own a sense of destiny, and embrace it. He wants us to see the whole picture of how our life and our work fit it with His overall purposes for the world.

equipping ability
God desires us to be reproducing laborers and ministers, just as we have become ourselves. He wants us to train others with the skills and knowledge that we possess. We are more concerned now with multiplying workers than merely adding numbers to the Kingdom.

"He who does the work is not so profitably employed as he who multiplies the workers."

John R. Mott

(((CAUTION)))

It is easy to misunderstand this phase we all long to achieve. Often a pastor will jump from church to church, trying to find the perfect ministry match. Some will even move every 2-3 years. Unfortunately, this is not how most will arrive at Phase Five. Frequently, it is an internal move more than an external one which God requires.

the construction of a life...

Phase Five represents those components in a house that are personal finishing touches, and make the house novel and unique. They give it personality and flair. It might be adding a deck or some trim around the siding or even a patio or porch. Now—the house is complete. It is grand and enables the homeowner to enjoy all the years of labor that have been put into it.

your part

- Trust and rest in God's movement of your position (location and proximity).
- See God's hand in the midst of trials.
- Disciple and mentor others.
- Surround yourself with like visionaries.
- Work smarter rather than harder.
- Recognize humbly that it is God who has brought you this far.

reflect and respond...

Think of people you know who are in this phase of life. Describe the traits that they exhibit from the list of God's objectives. What do you admire most about them? How would you describe their life? Who of these might be able to mentor you in your current phase of life?

Phase Six: afterglow & anointing

This final phase is the ultimate goal for each one of us. It generally occurs in the twilight years of life when we are living from the overflow of our wisdom, experience and labor. In these final years, others simply want to be around you because of the life you have lived. There is great respect, admiration and influence that you carry. Think about older saints you know that have entered this phase. Do you know any? It seems to me that in the 1990s, Dr. Billy Graham entered this phase. He had lived his life so well, that all who knew him held him in high esteem and honor. While Phase Six is not necessarily synonymous with fame, it certainly means that you have great influence with those who do know you.

God's objectives for phase six...

influence

God desires us to hold a deep and wide span of influence. At this point, we naturally mentor. We may, perhaps, even mentor from far away (others may hear about our lives, hear a tape of us speaking, or read what we have written).

leadership production

God desires us to reproduce leaders who can lead as effectively as we have. This is the highest level of disciple-making and spiritual reproduction. Only a leader can reproduce another leader. This mentoring of other leaders becomes a fulfilling part of Phase Six.

fulfillment

God desires that we realize that the reward of life is the journey itself. At this point we find deep satisfaction in just *being* who we are and *doing* what we are doing.

anointing on life

We find ourselves walking in a life-style of blessing and anointing. The overflow of our lives impacts others, and we influence people without even trying.

the construction of a life...

By this final stage, you have grown through the other stages well. You now enjoy the results of years of quality "home improvements."

examples:

In ministry arena
Billy Graham
Bill Bright

In secular arena
Margaret Thatcher
Muhammad Ali

your part

- Select and mentor sharp, potential giants.
- Reflect His glory in everything.
- Communicate from the overflow – let your heart spill over

reflect and respond...

This final phase is all about finishing well. It's about a life well lived. Now give yourself the freedom to dream big. What is the vision for life that God has given you? Even if this vision is not absolutely clear to you, envision what your life might be like during this phase. Describe it.

Have you caught a glimpse of the big picture? This can be an overwhelming amount of information, but knowing the full panorama encourages us within each stage. Look ahead to the end phases anytime you become discouraged with the stage you are in right now. Be encouraged to persevere – God desires the end result for *all* His children!!!

PHASE-JUMPING...

It can be difficult to determine when we are moving from one stage to the next.
Below are some hints that may give us a clue that a transition is occurring:

Common boundaries that mark beginnings of new phases . . .	As you begin moving into new phases, you will notice . . .
Crisis/tests/breaking	You begin holding a different sphere of influence.
Promotions	You recognize the greater importance of people.
Learning a major, new concept	
A new ministry	You experience deeper tests of obedience and leadership.
Unusual experience	You become relevant to new audiences.
A life-changing encounter with someone	
Geographic move	Others sense and recognize your growth.
Experiencing divine guidance	

assess yourself . . .

Walk through the memories of your life. Write down major events, conversations, decisions, or ministry experiences where you settled certain issues in those seasons of your life. Reflect on where you think you are in the stages of growth described in this lesson.

What stage do you think you are in right now?

What are the issues God is wanting you to address?

do a time line...

Now that we have looked at each of the six phases, let's map out our personal growth. In each phase listed below, describe your growth (or lack of it) in the space provided. If you are past the phase, write about the experiences that brought you through it. If you are in the phase, write about what you are experiencing now. If you are not yet in the phase, evaluate what it will take for you to get there. Be sure to include the successes and struggles of each phase because both are part of the growth process. This exercise should take some time. It will be a great way to step back and really see the big picture.

phase one . . .

phase two . . .

phase three . . .

phase four . . .

phase five . . .

phase six . . .

bringing it all home...

Based on the information that you wrote about above. List three specific steps that you need to take to continue your growth process—either to work through a current phase or to head toward the next phase.

1._____

_____

2._____

_____

3._____

_____

I challenge you to finish this surgery that you have begun on yourself – to finish building the house of your life until it is complete and can stand up against the winds of adversity throughout life.

who do you think you are?

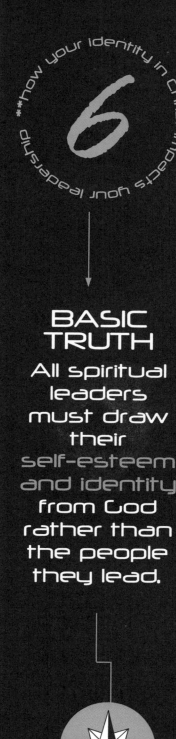

how your identity in Christ impacts your leadership

Albert Einstein, as a young man, was not considered especially bright. He certainly wasn't considered brilliant . . . in fact, as a boy, he actually flunked math class! One day, while standing in line to pay a certain type of tax, his mind wandered far away. After a brief wait, his turn came to pay his taxes. As he stepped up to face the clerk, she asked for his name. Einstein just stood there completely silent. Again, she started, "Sir, we are in a hurry, please, what is your name?" Silence. For the third time she impatiently sputtered, "Sir, we do not have time for games! Please, what is your name?" Finally, he confessed, "I'm so sorry, but for the life of me, I simply cannot remember!" He had to go back to the end of the line in hopes that he would remember the next time around. What irony! The man with the highest I.Q. in line that day couldn't remember who he was!

we're like einstein...

There's an analogy in that story for us. Albert Einstein suffered from something many Christians are plagued with today – we've forgotten our identity. We say the right phrases and we read the right words from the pages of the Bible, but deep down, we don't really know who we are.

This lesson is foundational to our personal and leadership development. As we work through this lesson, these truths have the potential to do the following:

- Change the way we live.
- Change the level of confidence we have in our leadership role.
- Enable us to put our emotional health, our personal security, and our identity into the hands of God, making us a more Christ-like influence.

the facts of the matter...

How we perceive ourselves is one of the determining factors of the quality of our leadership. Joyce Brothers insightfully noted, "You cannot consistently perform in a manner that is inconsistent with the way you see yourself."

- Our self-image is a barrier that must be raised for us to reach our potential.
- We must change our beliefs before we can change our behavior.
- We do not attempt greater things because it does not match our perceived mental image of who we are.

BASIC TRUTH

All spiritual leaders must draw their self-esteem and identity from God rather than the people they lead.

houston, i think we have a problem

Look at the diagram below. The top line represents our God-given potential and the bottom line represents our self-image – the way we see ourselves. The dotted line represents our usual level of behavior or performance. Notice that our performance usually hovers at the level of our self-image. Most of the time we go through life staying within our comfort zone. We tend to resist that which we think is above or below our view of ourselves. Every once in a while we become adventurous and pull off something that surprises us. But then we chalk it all up to luck, tell the story to everyone, and go on living at a level far below our potential. Compare that to the level of potential that we never reach! Certainly we will have good and bad days (the peak represents a good day) but we usually snap back to the level our self-image dictates.

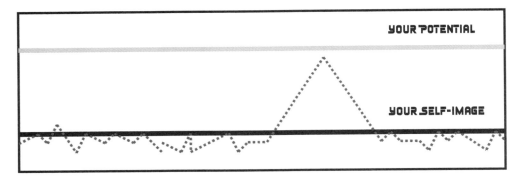

YOUR POTENTIAL

YOUR SELF-IMAGE

reflect and respond...

Write about any specific instances or seasons in your life when you have struggled with your self-image. What was the greatest challenge? How did you overcome it?

Write about one of your bursts of adventure and achievement, and how you were able to live closer to the level of your potential . . .

real life...

Between her low paying job and her low level of esteem, Phyllis' life spiraled down into welfare and depression. The only destiny she felt was the destiny of continuing in failure. But after reading a book called "Power of Believing," she decided to focus on the potential her life held. She evaluated herself to discover what she had to offer the world. Soon she recalled that as a school girl, she had an uncanny ability to make people laugh. She began focusing on this strength and her life was never the same. This woman, previously known as the "scrub lady," went on to be known as one of the most successful entertainers of her day. Her name? Comedienne Phyllis Dillar.

get rid of the commoners...

The problem of a low self-image does not happen all by itself. There are hundreds of reasons why different individuals struggle with issues of self-esteem. Listed below are some of the common contributors to a low self-image.

REASONS WHY WE'RE OFTEN DOWN ON OURSELVES:

we live in a negative society.
For example, most news on TV is bad news. Even the weather is profiled negatively. We say there is a 20% chance of rain, rather than an 80% chance of sunshine.

we have had our abilities questioned by others.
Negative words are easily recalled. Positive words are barely remembered. Behavioral scientists have said it takes 14 compliments to displace one criticism.

we confuse failure in a project with failure in life.
We fail at one venture, and we say, "I'm a failure," instead of realizing, "I have failed in one area."

We often waste time and fail to complete tasks.
Feeling unworthy, we procrastinate on attempting tough challenges. This leads to further discouragement.

We make unrealistic and unfair comparisons with other's physical features or personal experiences.
We tend to compare our worst with someone else's best.

We often have untrained memories.
Feeling as though you have a bad memory is a chief cause of a poor self image.

We fail to take care of ourselves.
It's a vicious circle. When we get depressed about something, we often fail to take care or ourselves, which leads to a diminishing self esteem. We feel unworthy.

We set unrealistic/unreachable standards of perfection.
Sometimes the standards for our appearance (from Hollywood) or for our intelligence (from Harvard) sets us up for failure. In reality, we can never be perfect.

We feel that we don't excel at something.
We look at the worst of ourselves and are never satisfied with the accomplishments and successes that we have achieved. This is often caused by unfair comparison.

our four images

The truth is, all of us carry the baggage of not one image, but four. We tend to relate to people and conduct ourselves based upon one of the images we are aware of at the moment. Note the diagram below and see how I have listed those images.

Image 4: The image others have of us.
Image 3: The image we try to project to others.
Image 2: The image we actually have of ourselves.
Image 1: The image God has of us.

Our job in this chapter is to peel back the three outward layers — and live from our true identity: God's image of us!

reflect and respond...

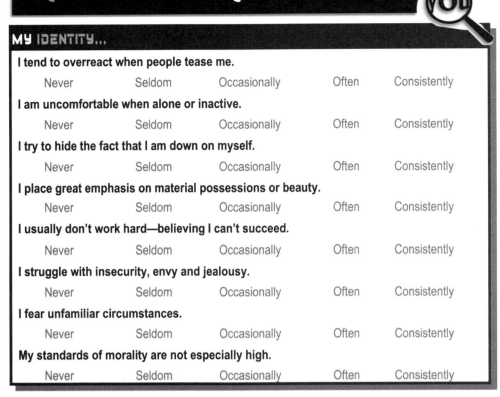

MY IDENTITY...

I tend to overreact when people tease me.				
Never	Seldom	Occasionally	Often	Consistently
I am uncomfortable when alone or inactive.				
Never	Seldom	Occasionally	Often	Consistently
I try to hide the fact that I am down on myself.				
Never	Seldom	Occasionally	Often	Consistently
I place great emphasis on material possessions or beauty.				
Never	Seldom	Occasionally	Often	Consistently
I usually don't work hard—believing I can't succeed.				
Never	Seldom	Occasionally	Often	Consistently
I struggle with insecurity, envy and jealousy.				
Never	Seldom	Occasionally	Often	Consistently
I fear unfamiliar circumstances.				
Never	Seldom	Occasionally	Often	Consistently
My standards of morality are not especially high.				
Never	Seldom	Occasionally	Often	Consistently

Which of the above do you see as weaknesses in your life? Do you notice any other weaknesses not listed above? Write about it.

let the change begin...

Now that we have recognized some of the misconceptions we have about ourselves, let's remember the truth that God reveals in His word. What we need to do is change the picture we have of ourselves based on the picture of us that God revealed in the New Testament. The truth presented in this text will radically change how we approach our Christian lives.

it's gotta be an inside job...

Look at the scripture on the right, 2 Corinthians 5.16-18. Paul is giving us a snapshot of who we are. Think about it, when we asked Christ to come into our lives, we didn't change physically – our height, weight, and physical characteristics all remained. Instead, what was dramatically changed was the spirit inside of us. He changes the part of us that is eternal. God did an inside job on us. When God saved us, the purpose was to give us a whole new dimension to our identity. We are not just "sinners" saved by grace. We are new creatures in Christ!

Unfortunately, even though we believe God did an inside job on us, most of us don't live by that foundation. Instead, we continue to view life through a very human perspective. Let's look at our human way of thought in comparison to our Father in heaven.

our perspective	God's perspective
We see life, limited by time and space – a day-to-day existence.	God sees the big picture – our lives in light of eternity!
Life is based upon our experience.	Life is based upon our position in Christ.
We see our flaws and lots of room to grow.	God sees the beauty of His children, complete in Christ.

if you could only have 3 things

As we begin to think of our lives in light of God's perspective we realize the limits we often place on ourselves. We long for the indomitable spirit of childhood when we "didn't know any better" than to believe we were special to God and to others.

A little girl stood by the window during a terrible thunderstorm, smiling every time the lightning flashed. Her perplexed father finally asked what she was doing. She giggled, "I think that God's trying to take my picture!"

She understood that her heavenly Father loves her deeply – something we often forget. Not only does God loves us but He has also given us some amazing gifts. As we just read in 2 Corinthians, God has made us "new creatures." The newness comes with some great benefits! Let's look at three things God has given us: new positions, new possessions and new potential.

God's perspective:
2 Corinthians 5.16-18

"Because of this decision we don't evaluate people by what they have or how they look. We looked at the Messiah that way once and got it all wrong, as you know. We certainly don't look at him that way anymore. Now we look inside, and what we see is that anyone united with the Messiah get a fresh start, is created new. The old is gone; a new life burgeons! Look at it! All this comes from God who settled the relationship between us and him, and then called us to settle our relationships with each other."

(THE MESSAGE)

new position

Read the scripture on the left again. We are called "new creations" when we are placed in Christ. Something fundamentally changes inside. No longer must we live merely based upon our life on earth, with its ups and downs. We can live based upon our position in Christ.

God's perspective:
2 Corinthians 5.17

"Therefore, if anyone is in Christ, he is a new creation; the old has gone, the new has come! All this is from God..."

(NIV)

real life...

There was a man who made his living by selling helium balloons on the streets of New York City. Whenever business began to die down he would send one of his colorful balloons zipping into the air and then business would begin to pick up again. One particularly slow day, he let go of several balloons: a red, yellow, and white balloon. It didn't take long before he felt a little tug on his pant leg. Looking down, he discovered a little African-American boy standing there. With child-like innocence he said, "Mister, I have a question . . . if you let go of a black balloon would it go up too?" The man knew just what this boy was getting at. With wisdom beyond his years he bent down and said, "Son, listen to me, it's what is *inside* those balloons that makes them go up."

what the greeks have to say...

When the Bible tells us that we are new creations, it truly means it. The Greek word for new creation ("new creature" in some versions) literally means "a new species of being that has never existed on earth before." Think about that! When we ask God to come into our lives, it's like God does spiritual surgery. He cuts us open and changes our very being. Therefore, we are a new race – Christians! We must not simply be aware of our new position, we must wholeheartedly embrace it. God wants to infiltrate this planet with a whole new race of people. Not Anglos, Hispanics, Asians or Africans, but a new breed called "new creatures in Christ!" Think about how your life might change if you really believed in your new identity!

real life...

Victor was five years old when his family defected to the United States from the Soviet Union. His parents enrolled him in kindergarten right away, but since he didn't know English very well, he started struggling in school. Teachers started throwing Victor into remedial classes and classmates quickly pegged him as a "stupid idiot." It didn't take long for the little boy to agree with this identity.

As a sophomore in high school, Victor's teacher advised him to drop out of school. Her reasoning was straightforward, "You are just slowing everyone else down, you are never going to amount to anything. You might as well just get a job and try to make ends meet." So, Victor did. He dropped out of school at 16 years old and began to work odd jobs.

Then something wonderful happened. Fourteen years later, at age thirty, Victor happened to take an IQ test. He discovered that he had an IQ of 161 . . . he was a genius! From that point on, things changed. Since then, Victor has written two books, patented several inventions, and has a wonderful family. He is a new man.

Think about it. The **only thing** about Victor that changed was the way he saw himself. His IQ didn't change, but when he got up in the morning and looked at himself in the mirror, he didn't see a dunce anymore—he saw a genius. What might happen if every morning you woke up and saw a "new creature in Christ" instead of the same old creature, living a mediocre life and having a bad hair day?

God made you a new creature and gave you a new position in Him. Take a moment to compare where you were (or where you would be) without your new position. How has your life changed since you became a new creature? (My worth is determined by the people I spend time with. vs. My worth is dependent on God's past choice to love and accept me.)

my old thoughts about my identity . . .   my new thoughts about my identity . . .

new possessions

In 2 Corinthians 5.17-18, it says "the old things have passed away and the new things have come. All these things are form God." What old and new things is Paul talking about? Read 2 Peter 1.3-4 printed on the right.

Did you catch it? Peter says God has given us "everything" we need to live out our calling. We have the opportunity to "participate in the divine nature" so that we can be like Jesus. God doesn't want us to merely *exist* as Christians so we can get into heaven. He wants to make us look like Jesus so we can *fit into* heaven. We touched on this diagram earlier, but in this chapter we're going to go deeper into the topic of our identity. This diagram displays some of the key "resources" or "equipment" God has placed inside of you: Study it.

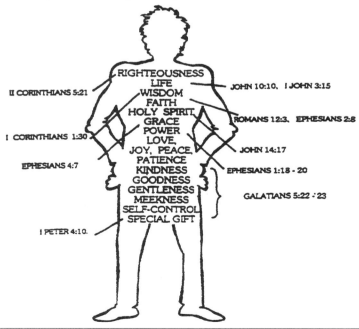

God's perspective: 2 Peter 1.3-4

His divine power has given us everything we need for life and godliness through our knowledge of Him who called us by His own glory and goodness. Through these He has given us His very great and precious promises, so that through them you may participate in the divine nature and escape the corruption in the world caused by evil desires."

(NIV)

This diagram is a great thing to hang on the bathroom mirror so you can remember who you are each morning. Confess each "resource" and scripture aloud. Some think this is brain washing. I agree . . . it sure is! Let's wash our brains clean of the junk that the world has told us and remember the possessions that God has given us.

real life...

During my college years, I worked as a youth pastor at a little church near the university. I deeply wanted to reach high school students. I felt like God had given me a vision to create a multi-media production for schools that would both entertain and spark discussion about the Bible. Unfortunately, I had no money to buy the equipment for all of this.

One night, I sat on my bed, whining to God that I couldn't pay for this great idea. In response, God impressed me with the fact that He had already given me every resource I needed to accomplish this goal. It wasn't about money at that point, it was about the gifts that He had put inside of me that lay dormant. As I continued to pray, God reminded me that I was in college on an art scholarship. Then, the idea struck me. I was to take my portfolio of cartoons and drawings, show them to various newspaper editors in the area, and propose an idea. I would draw editorial cartoons for them on local issues for $10 each. All of the local papers were buying nationally syndicated cartoons from well known artists. I would provide cartoons on local and state issues. Hmmm. The idea might just work.

The next week, after more prayer, I put a tie on, grabbed my portfolio and went out to four newspaper publishers . Much to my surprise, each of them said, "Yes!" Soon, more papers jumped on board. Each week, I sat down to create a cartoon and send it out to these papers. I had my own little syndicate. Needless to say, before the year was over, I had all the money I needed to buy the multi-media equipment and fulfill the ministry I felt called to do.

In a similar way, these "resources" inside of every new creature are there to accomplish something. Inside you, God put love, faith, power, spiritual gifts, etc. You don't need to beg for more! You have everything you need to fulfill your calling and influence others.

reflect and respond...

God will do extraordinary things through ordinary people who will start believing these truths about themselves. What might God be able to do through your life when you begin to accept and believe these truths? (give me the courage to share my faith, risk failure, etc.) List one step of obedience you could take.

We each have the same number of muscles in our bodies, but we may not be able to demonstrate the same amount of strength. Why? Because, we have not taken the time to *develop* our muscles. In the same way, each Christian has the same amount of possessions as every other believer, but we don't all demonstrate the same spiritual strength. Why? We have not *developed* them! Review the list of possessions that God has given us. Which ones are strongly apparent in your life? Which do you need to embrace because they are absent in your life?

rewind <<<

Describe what your new position in Christ means to you.

 HALF TIME...continue the chapter next meeting

rewind <<<

God has made us "new creature" and because of that he has given us a new position in Him and He has given us new possessions. But that's not all, God has also given us a new potential. Let's take a look...

new potential

There is a third truth we learn from this test in II Corinthians 5.16-18. As a new creature, God wants us to step into a life of ministry. We all are supposed to have some kind of ministry, regardless of our occupation. Each of us is responsible to advance the kingdom. Paul calls it the ministry of reconciliation. Verse 18 tells us that God has given us the ministry of reconciliation.

Could you imagine a giant train engine pulling only one small car on a long journey? It would not be a good use of time and energy since the engine has much more potential than it is using. In the same way, it is foolish for us, as Christians, to use our great potential to only warm a pew on Sundays. We need to take people with us as we journey through this life to the gates of heaven. We have the power to not only get to heaven ourselves, but to take a whole lot of other people with us.

real life...

There is a phenomenon among my family's pets. Otis, the cat, had been a part of my aunt and uncle's household for quite some time before Pierre came on the scene. Pierre, the puppy, was a little, perky toy poodle. Otis didn't know what to make of this new hyper playmate, so he tried to avoid him. But Pierre didn't have any other friends, so about two weeks into his stay, my relatives started noticing the dog was following the cat everywhere . . . Otis would jump on the couch, Pierre would jump on the couch. Otis would hop on the counter, Pierre would hop on the counter. Otis would climb a tree, Pierre would *climb a tree!*

My uncle was confused because, "dogs don't climb trees." Then it finally hit him: Pierre thought he was a cat! He had never known another dog before, so he assumed that he was just a younger version of Otis! That's the power of believing! That's the power of a strong sense of identity!

**God's perspective
2 Corinthians 5.18**

"All this is from God, who reconciled us to Himself through Christ and gave us the ministry of reconciliation."

(NIV)

87

the average child...

I don't cause teachers trouble
My grades have been okay
I keep up on my chores at home
I'm in school everyday

My teachers think I'm average
My parents think so too
I wish I didn't know that
Cause there's things I'd like to do

I'd like to build a rocket ship
I've got a book that shows you how
Or start a stamp collection
Well, no use in trying now

'Cause, since I know I'm average
I'm just smart enough you see
To know there's nothing special
I should expect of me

I'm just part of that majority
That bump part of the bell
Who live their lives unnoticed
In an average kind of hell.

That is NOT the way it has to be! Being a new creature and believing we are new creatures should dramatically change our lives.

real life...

Think about The Emancipation Proclamation. Its purpose was to free all of the slaves in the South. Yet, were all the slaves freed immediately after it was written? No, the Civil War continued for two more years. Even then, it wasn't until 100 years later, when the civil rights movement began, that this freedom started to become a reality. People had to stand up and say, "I am free and I will be free!" Likewise, we need to believe that we are free in Christ. Scripture is our emancipation proclamation. We need to stand up and claim our identity in Him.

reflect and respond...

Based on your identity in Christ, what do you declare your freedom from today? (perfectionism, fear, addiction)

now what?

Now that we have recognized that God has given us a new position, possessions, and potential, we must do something with that knowledge. Let's look at three action steps to take to become the "new creatures" that God intends for us to be.

1. renew our perspective

When we sin, we begin to get extremely down on ourselves. After we have committed the same sin several times, we can assume God doesn't even want to hear from us anymore. We think that He is sick of hearing our confessions again and again. Instead, as a new creation, we should acknowledge our sin, thank Him for His forgiveness and begin to confess our new identity. It is not natural for our new nature to sin, but we still struggle with the flesh and our minds battle to go back to the old programming we have previously lived with. However, we are not our old sinful selves . . . we are new creatures. We must think like new creatures.

reflect and respond...

What sins are you confessing that continue to be a struggle? What hurdles that you have already written about need a new perspective? Write down the old perspective that you had and the new perspective you have now as a "new creature."

2. Release our past

We must let go of our old patterns, sins, bad habits and relationships. This is the part that is often the hardest because it means letting go of what is familiar. Our identity cannot be attached to our past experience. It must be tied to our present position in Him. Our behavior must follow our belief.

reflect and respond...

Make a list of your old patterns, habits and relationships. Of these lifestyle ingredients, which do you believe is hindering your growth as a "new creature"? How will you strip them from your life?

Not only can deep-rooted patterns of sin haunt us, but also past wrongs and events can scar us. Will you also release those to God? (Even the hurt, bitterness, resentment, fear?)

We must begin to see our life from God's perspective.

Our worst sins arise as our response to our innate human fear that we are nobody.

3. remember your purpose

We must remember why God left us in this world! We must embrace His purpose for our lives if we're going to experience the power inside us! Ultimately, God's purpose is for us to build the kingdom and advance the cause of Christ. This purpose is the most important business that we can be about. And we will never fully experience our identity in Christ and the fulfillment that comes from the realization of what we were created to do until we pursue this purpose. That doesn't mean that we have to drop all of our plans and start a church in Zimbabwe, but it does mean that we have to uncover and live out our God-given purpose — and realize how our purpose fits into God's great purpose for the whole world.

real life...

Four year old Todd worshipped the ground his dad walked on. In fact, every night when dad came home from work, Todd would cling to him and yell, "Daddy, let's play!"
One particular night when his dad returned, Todd ran up and exclaimed his usual greeting. Yet dad had brought home two briefcases full of work to do and he just didn't have time to play with his son. So he tried to cut a deal with the little boy.
  "Todd, I'll tell you what. I don't have time to play tonight, but I'll read you a bed-time story later."
  But Todd would not give up, so finally Dad came up with an idea. He swiped a newspaper from the floor and noticed a travel agent ad. A picture of the world was splashed across the ad. He ripped up the picture, sprinkled it on the carpet and said, "Todd, I want you to pretend like that's a puzzle. And when you put that picture of the world back together, I'll play a game with you." He thought he was safe for at least 2 or 3 hours.
  Fifteen minutes later, Todd was back. "Dad, let's play a game now." Sure enough, little Todd had put that whole picture together again. He exclaimed, "Todd, how did you do that so quickly?" Innocently, Todd said: "Dad, it was simple, I noticed on the back of the picture of the world, there was a picture of the man. I found out that when I got the man right, the world was right."

The same is true for us. If we want to transform our world, we must first be transformed ourselves!

reflect and respond...

What do you believe God's purpose for the world is? What do you believe is God's specific purpose for your life? How does your purpose fit in with God's overriding purpose?

assess yourself...

As new creatures in Christ, God has given us a new

P_____

P_____

P_____

Which of these three is making the biggest impact on you right now? Why?

Go back to the introduction of this lesson where you wrote about weaknesses in the area of your self-image. Look at those in the light of the "new creature" that God made you. What will you do to change your thinking? (If you need help changing your thinking, look back at the "How to step into the truth" section in the last half of the Security or Sabotage lesson.)

bringing it all home...

In the end, our worst fears are not that we cannot do something significant. Our worst fears are that we might actually be someone and have something to offer that could change this world. This represents such a weight to us that we choose not to bear it, instead, living at a level far beneath our potential.

Nelson Mandela

A new habit to begin:

Attempt something every week in your life that you could not possibly pull off without God.

% this is a test %

life's pop quizzes that prove our leadership potential and maturity

My Spanish teacher in college was a sweet, older lady who seemed more like a grandmother than a professor. Every Friday she would give us a quiz. But before she would hand it out she would say, "Kids, I really don't want to give you this test, but it's the only way we're going to know if you're ready for next year." It was obvious that she really didn't want to put us through the experience, but she knew that she had to test us in order to do her job and to get the results she needed.

As I remember my experience with that professor, I can't help but liken it to my relationship with God. I wonder if that is the same heart posture that God assumes as we struggle through the tests of life. I don't think God finds joy in throwing us into struggles. I believe He would say to us, "I don't want to give you this test but it's the only way you're going to be able to demonstrate whether you're ready for the challenges ahead." Testing is the pathway to growth and progress.

another test?

Tests are common to all of us. In order to graduate into the third grade, we must pass the tests of second grade. All of the appliances we own in our homes have gone through comprehensive testing before they make their way out into the showrooms. It's the same with automobiles. Nearly every part of a new car is drug through intensive tests for safety and performance. Furthermore, you'd never buy a car without taking it out on a "test drive" yourself. Why then would it surprise us that God would also have a series of tests for his children to go through to demonstrate their maturity and potential?

abraham and isaac

Read Genesis 22.1-2, 9-13.

In this classic text, Abraham is ushered into a "test of faith." It is clear from the passage, as well as the New Testament commentary in the book of Hebrews, that God did not intend to have Issac executed. It was merely a test for his father, a test that he passed with flying colors, proving he had settled the issue of obedience and Lordship.

Look again at verse 12
"'Do not lay a hand on the boy," he said. "Do not do anything to him. For now I know that you fear God, because you have not withheld from me your son, your only son.'" (NIV)

God already knew Abraham would be faithful because God is omniscient. So, he did not need to test Abraham to find out whether he would be faithful. Instead, it was a test for Abraham to **experientially** prove that he was who he claimed to be. It was time for him to demonstrate with his life what he said with his lips!

93

reflect and respond...

Do you feel like you are being tested right now in any areas of your life? What have you learned through past times of testing?

define it...

So, what exactly is a test? In this lesson we define it as:

an opportunity which challenges us to experientially prove our potential and maturity.

Working through theses challenges that we call "tests" will usually reveal one of three results indicating your inward potential and maturity:

POVERTY	PLATEAU	PROGRESS
This is identified when you realize that no growth has occurred and you are doing worse than the previous time	This is revealed happens when you realize that you have not grown at all since the last time you were tested in this area.	This becomes clear when you realize that you have grown and responded better since the last time you were tested in this

Before you read any further, stop and notice the five truths about testing listed to the left. These are foundational to our understanding of leadership tests.

what is common to man...

Since we know that we will encounter testing in our lives, it is helpful to understand several different kinds of tests that we can expect. The material you're about to read was inspired by Kevin Gerald, pastor of Covenant Celebration Church in Tacoma, WA. I am grateful for his insight.

This chapter will walk you through ten different tests that you will experience at some time in your life and leadership. At the conclusion of each of the ten tests you will have an opportunity to evaluate your personal growth on the poverty-plateau-progress scale. Take some time to reflect and let God to speak to you in these areas of your life.

TEN TESTS THAT PROVE OUR POTENTIAL AND MATURITY

1. The test of small things

This test proves our faithfulness and reveals our potential for greater opportunities and challenges.

God challenges us to be faithful with the small things before He entrusts us with bigger things. David was faithful as a shepherd by defending his flock against a bear and a lion. God didn't send David out against Goliath without any experience. David had to learn to be faithful with sheep before he was ready to tackle a giant! The issue was not David's ability or potential. It was seeing if he would faithfully execute the assignment, regardless of its size.

your test...

See if any of these are true in your life . . .

- Maybe He has called you to be faithful as a follower before you try to be the leader.
- Maybe you need to work in a lower position before you may be trusted with a promotion.
- Maybe you need to use the gifts you have before God multiplies those gifts.
- Maybe you need to learn to be a good steward of your small income before God blesses you with a pay raise.
- Maybe you need to learn to be content to be single before God allows you to have an intimate relationship.

Think about the ways that God may be calling you to be faithful in the smaller things of life. The real battle is perspective. You must *choose* to treat both the small and large things as important resources in your life.

reflect and respond...

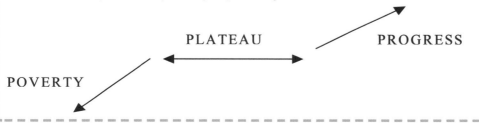

What "small things" are testing you in your life right now?

In what ways can you *choose* to think differently about these things?

Rate yourself on the poverty-plateau-progress scale regarding the test of small things. Place an "X" at the place where you see your personal growth.

PLATEAU   PROGRESS

POVERTY

Fact

The size of something does not necessarily indicate it's worth!

God's perspective
Luke 16.10
"Unless you are faithful in small matters, you won't be faithful in large ones. If you cheat even a little, you won't be honest with greater responsibilities."

Ephesians 5.16a
"Make the most of every opportunity."

(NLT)

God's perspective: Matthew 6.6

"But when you pray, go away by yourself, shut the door behind you, and pray to your Father secretly. Then your Father, who knows all secrets, will reward you."

(NLT)

Job 1.8-12

"Then the Lord said to Satan, "Have you notice my servant Job? He is the finest man in all the earth—a man of complete integrity. He fears God and will have nothing to do with evil."
Satan replied to the Lord, "Yes, Job fears God, but not without good reason! You have always protected him and his home and his property from harm. You have made him prosperous in everything he does. Look how rich he is! But take away everything he has, and he will surely curse you to your face!"
"All right, you may test him," the Lord said to Satan. "Do whatever you want with everything he possesses, but don't harm him physically." So Satan left the Lord's presence.

(NLT)

2. The motivation test

This test comes to those who are doing right, to reveal *why* they are doing it.

Jesus was consumed with the issue of motives. He spoke of motives regarding prayer and fasting often. Read Matthew 6.5-18.

This test comes very quietly and secretly. God begins to nudge your heart and no one else knows that you are experiencing it. He wants to purify your motives not just your behavior. We can never be faultless—but we can be blameless. This has to do with our heart and our motives. Why is this so crucial?

BECAUSE WHY YOU DO SOMETHING WILL ULTIMATELY DETERMINE WHAT YOU DO.

real life...

It was a hard blow for Samuel Brengle when he found himself in a cellar shining the boots of other cadets. He had not expected this. When signing up for the Salvation Army, Brengle had expected to be thrown immediately into evangelistic ministry. Instead, he found himself surrounded by a pile of black, muddy shoes. It was a sharp temptation for Brengle to see this as a blatant waste of his time and talent. He asked Jesus if he was burying his talents. He wondered if he was wasting his time in the Salvation Army.

It was down in that cellar that he saw a vision. In it, Jesus, the central figure, was washing disciples' feet! Jesus, the One who had existed in the glories of the Everlasting Father, was now kneeling at the feet of grimy, uneducated fishermen . . . all to wash their feet!

With this change of mind, Brengle's heart bowed low. He pledged to the Savior: "Lord, you washed their feet, so I will shine their boots. And with that, he went forth, polishing boots with an enthusiasm in his arms, a song on his lips, and a peace in his heart.

Years later he recorded: "I had fellowship with Jesus every morning that week while down in the cellar . . . My prayer was, 'Dear Lord, let me serve the servants of Jesus. That is sufficient for me!'"

reflect and respond...

Take a few moments to ask God to search your heart as you examine your motives. What areas of your life are being tested to reveal your motivation? What motives are fueling your leadership? Your life?

Rate yourself on the poverty-plateau-progress scale regarding the motivation test.
Place an "X" at the place where you see your personal growth.

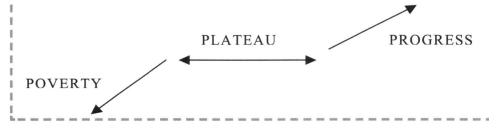

PLATEAU   PROGRESS

POVERTY

3. The stewardship test

This test proves how strategically and generously we handle resources that we presently control.

When we think of stewardship, money may come to mind but it is a deeper issue than that. Stewardship also includes our time, resources, relationships, and many other areas. With every resource we have, large or small, we must *choose* to be a good steward and be faithful to the One who gave the gift. God's question for us is: Whatcha gonna do with watcha got?

real life...

A young man felt called to reach the world for Christ and wanted to be a missionary in a foreign country. After training for mission work, he married a beautiful young woman, and together they left for Africa to begin their ministry. But soon after they arrived, he made the horrible discovery that his wife was too fragile and too physically sick to live in such a primitive environment. This discovery forced them to return home. Naturally, this man was devastated! Yet, he made a very wise decision—he recognized this was a test. He made a conscious decision to be as faithful as he possibly could right where he was. He took over his father's small business of making unfermented wine for church communion services and built it up—in fact, you have probably had his grape juice. His name is Welch. Because of his business, Mr. Welch has given hundreds of thousands of dollars to world missions. He has done much more as a sender than he ever could have done on the mission field himself!

reflect and respond...

In what areas are you already a good steward?

In what areas of your life could you be a better steward? What needs to be done to improve in these areas?

Rate yourself on the poverty-plateau-progress scale regarding the stewardship test. Place an "X" at the place where you see your personal growth.

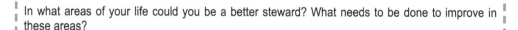

PLATEAU   PROGRESS

POVERTY

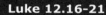

God's perspective:
Matthew 25.21
"The master was full of praise. 'Well done, my good and faithful servant. You have been faithful in handling this small amount, so now I will give you many more responsibilities. Let's celebrate together.'"

(NLT)

Luke 12.16-21
Then He told them this story: "The farm of a certain rich man produced a terrific crop. He talked to himself: 'What can I do? My barn isn't big enough for this harvest.' Then he said, 'Here's what I'll do: I'll tear down my barns and build bigger ones. Then I'll gather in all my grain and goods, and I'll say to myself, "Self, you've done well! You've got it made and can now retire. Take it easy and have the time of you life!"'

"Just then God showed up and said, 'Fool! Tonight you die. And your barnful of goods—who gets it?'

"That's what happens when you fill your barn with Self and not with God."

(THE MESSAGE)

4. The wilderness test

This test comes in a time of dryness to reveal our potential for change and to enter a new growth level.

Often, the wilderness test comes upon us subtly. The passion diminishes from our lives like a slow tire leak. Reading the Bible becomes about as much fun as reading the phone book. We get stuck.

This test is a challenge to join God on a deeper level, living from *character,* not *feelings.* During this testing time, we must face a decision. Will we keep doing what we know is right even when the "feelings" are not there to make the experience exciting? Or will we bend in the wilderness, assuming the cause is not worth the fight?

from the book...

In this passage, Moses is challenging the children of Israel to remember and obey God.

"Do not forget that He led you through the great and terrifying wilderness with poisonous snakes and scorpions, where it was so hot and dry. He gave you water from the rock! He fed you with manna in the wilderness, a food unknown to your ancestors. He did this to humble you and test you for your own good. He did it so you would never think that it was your own strength and energy that made you wealthy. Always remember that it is the Lord your God who gives you power to become rich, and He does it to fulfill the covenant He made with your ancestors."

Deuteronomy 8.15-18

reflect and respond...

Think back to a time in your life where you experienced the "wilderness test." Write about it here.

WHAT WAS THE STRUGGLE?	HOW WAS GOD FAITHFUL?	WHAT DID YOU LEARN?

If you feel like you are going through the wilderness test right now, ask God to reveal the deeper level that He is calling you to in your life. Ask others to pray for you as you work through this test. Two people that I will ask to pray for me:

_____

_____

**God's perspective:
Psalm 4.1-4**

"Answer me when I call, O God who declares me innocent. Take away my distress, Have mercy on me and hear my prayer. How long will you people ruin my reputation? How long will you make these groundless accusations? How long will you pursue lies? You can be sure of this: The LORD has set apart the godly for himself, the Lord will answer when I call to him. Don't sin by letting anger gain control over you. Think about it overnight and remain silent."

(NLT)

5. The credibility test

This test reveals our integrity and proves our ability to hold uncompromising ethics under pressure.

This test may come in the form of an ethical decision to be made . . . or it may be an issue when God asks, "who is going to do this and who is going to get the credit for it — you or Me?" Often in life we are tempted to compromise our beliefs or force the momentum instead of allowing God to do His work.

Read: 1 Samuel 16.7 and Galatians 2.11-14

real life...

I had an unusual hobby of witnessing to celebrities when I was in college. On one occasion I felt led to share with Olivia Newton John. So I headed over to one of her concerts and slipped back stage where I waited for her just outside her dressing room. My plan was simple; as soon as she came out I would share a few words with her and leave a tract for her to read. All was going on schedule until a bouncer noticed I was missing a back stage pass. After reasoning with him for a few minutes, he decided to let me stay—but only if I paid his bribe. I happened to have that exact amount with me and was seriously considering reaching for my wallet when God spoke to my heart and let me know that He had other plans. As I began to walk away in absolute discouragement, I suddenly heard someone calling my name. I turned around to find a long-lost friend who just happened to work back stage! He was able to connect me with Olivia's right hand man who agreed to let me speak with her. Olivia Newton John heard the gospel that night! Yet, my greatest lesson that night was yielding to let God pull it off, not me.

That was a test for me. If I had paid the bribe *I* would have gotten the glory. Yet, by trusting God and allowing *Him* to do His work, God got the glory.

reflect and respond...

What credibility tests have you encountered recently?

Where do you struggle most to maintain your integrity?

We must take deliberate steps to destroy the weaknesses in our lives. In the area of credibility, it is essential to have *deliberate accountability*. Take a moment to think of what areas you need accountability in and think of who should keep you accountable.
Who would be a good person? _____
When can I meet with them? _____
What specifics do I need to share with them?

Rate yourself on the poverty-plateau-progress scale regarding the credibility test.
Place an "X" at the place where you see your personal growth.

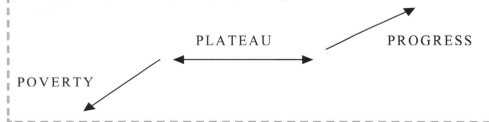

PLATEAU   PROGRESS

POVERTY

**God's perspective:
Galatians 2.11-14**
" Later when Peter came to Antioch, I had a face-to-face confrontation with him because he was clearly out of line. Here's the situation. Earlier, before certain persons had come from James, Peter regularly ate with the non-Jews. But, when that conservative group came from Jerusalem, he cautiously pulled back and put as much distance as he could manage between himself and his non-Jewish friends. That's how fearful he was of the conservative Jewish clique that's been pushing the old system of circumcision. Unfortunately, the rest of the Jews in the Antioch church joined in that hypocrisy so that even Barnabas was swept along in the charade."

(THE MESSAGE)

I Samuel 16.7

"But the Lord said to Samuel, 'Don't judge by his appearance or height, for I have rejected him. The Lord doesn't make decisions the way you do! People judge by outward appearance, but the Lord looks at a person's thoughts and intentions.'"

(NLT)

- The test of small things
- The motivation test
- The stewardship test
- The wilderness test
- The credibility test

reflect and respond...

When God tests us it isn't just for the fun of it! There is something that we need to learn or experience, or possibly an area that we need to trust God in or grow in. Often, it means that we need to *do* something about it, even if it's difficult. In light of what you are experiencing, what action(s) do you need to take? When will you do these things?

rewind <<<

Take a moment to review each of the five tests we've learned so far. Which test are you currently passing with flying colors? Which test are you failing at?

 HALF TIME...continue the chapter next meeting

rewind <<<

Testing is usually not enjoyable but it is necessary so that we can determine our level of growth. We have already learned about the test of small things, motivation, stewardship, wilderness, and credibility the test. Now let's take a look at a few more...

6. The authority test

This test reveals our attitude and willingness to submit to God-given authority.

As leaders, we must learn to submit to the authority of others . . . otherwise we have no right to ask others to submit to *us* as leaders. Authority is different than influence. Authority is given by God. Influence is earned by the leader. We must submit to leaders not because they earn it, but because God calls us to do so. No leader has any real influence unless he or she has proven himself or herself worthy of it in the eyes of the people.

from the **book...**

At the place where the road passes some sheepfolds, Saul went into a cave to relieve himself. But as it happened, David and his men were hiding in that very cave!

"Now's your opportunity!" David's men whispered to him. "Today is the day the Lord was talking about when He said, 'I will certainly put Saul in your power, to do with as you wish.'" Then David crept forward and cut off a piece of Saul's robe.

But then David's **conscience** began bothering him because he had cut Saul's robe. "The Lord knows **I shouldn't have done it**," he said to his men. "It is a **serious thing** to attack the Lord's anointed one, for the Lord himself has chosen him." So David sharply rebuked his men and did not let them kill Saul . . . . And [Saul] said to David, "You are a better man than I am, for you have repaid me good for evil. Yes, you have been wonderfully kind to me today, for when the Lord put me in a place where you could have killed me, you didn't do it. Who else would let his enemy get away when he had him in his power? May the Lord reward you well for the kindness you have shown me today. And now I realize that **you are surely going to be KING**, and Israel will flourish under you rule."

1 Samuel 24.3-7a, 17-20 (NIV)

reflect and **respond...**

What is your attitude to those in authority?

In what areas of your life are you a . . .

Leader	Follower
_____	_____
_____	_____
_____	_____
_____	_____

"Forgiveness is not an occasional act, it is a permanent attitude."

Martin Luther King, Jr.

God's Perspective: Hebrews 12.14-15
"Try to live in peace with everyone, and seek to live a clean and holy life, for those who are not holy will not see the Lord. Look after each other so that none of you will miss out on the special favor of God. Watch out that no bitter root of unbelief rises up among you, for whenever it springs up, many are corrupted by its poison."

(NLT)

Mark 11.25-26
"But when you are praying, first forgive anyone you are holding a grudge against, so that your Father in heaven will forgive your sins, too. But, if you do not forgive, neither will your father who is in heaven forgive your sins."

7. The offense test

This test comes to prove that we are not easily offended and that we are ready to forgive others.

Leaders, to a certain extent, must possess a thick skin—not a callused skin, but a thick skin. At times we will be criticized by both those we lead and our peers. Jesus possessed the perfect balance of toughness and tenderness. Even while he was dying, hanging on a cross, he still forgave those who had crucified him. Moments before he died Jesus said, "Father, forgive these people, because they don't know what they are doing." (Luke 23.34)

Leaders will likely face this test more often than anyone else. Why? Because leaders are the point people who are responsible for what happens in an organization. As leaders, we will incur more criticism, more attacks, more misunderstandings, and more gossip—simply because the buck stops with us!

real life...

During the Civil War, General Whiting was jealous of General Robert E. Lee and consequently spread many rumors about him. The time came when General Lee had a chance to settle the score. President Jefferson Davis was considering Whiting for a key promotion. He wanted to know what General Lee thought of Whiting. Without hesitation, Lee commended Whiting in the highest manner. Every officer present was astonished. One of them asked Lee after the interview if he had forgotten all the unkind words Whiting had spread about him. Lee responded, "I understand that the President wanted to know my opinion of Whiting, not Whiting's opinion of me."

reflect and respond...

Take a moment to evaluate the relationships in your life. Who do you need to forgive? Who do you need to seek forgiveness from? When will you speak with this person to make your relationship right?

Rate yourself on the poverty-plateau-progress scale regarding the offense test. Place an "X" at the place where you see your personal growth.

PLATEAU   PROGRESS

POVERTY

Keep short accounts in life!

8. The warfare test

This test reveals what we will do when we are in God's will and experience adversity or opposition.

Simply because we are in God's will, doesn't mean that we won't experience adversity or opposition. When we look through the Bible, we find many men and women of God who endured and excelled despite great opposition. Both Moses and Jeremiah experienced adversity for much of their life, yet they both were in God's will and able to deeply impact the world around them. . .

from the book...

Then the Lord replied to me, "If racing against mere men makes you tired, how will you race against horses? If you stumble and fall on open ground, what will you do in the thickets near the Jordan?"

Jeremiah 12.5

real life...

Every year at our church in San Diego, we performed the "Living Christmas Tree." It was a huge production, and some years we made it fun by bringing in live animals for the nativity seen. Unfortunately, the live animals did not always behave as we would want them to during a performance. As you would probably guess, the animals had a few "accidents" at very inappropriate times! As the choir stage was laughing at the scenes before them, the director would scold, "Stay in character!" No matter how crazy things became on stage, it was imperative that the singers stayed in character.

And so it is with us. Life will throw us curve balls that we did not plan for. Yet, good or bad, God calls us to continue living as we know we should live. Our job is to follow the script (the scripture) and to stay in character!

reflect and respond...

Think back to a time in your life when you were faced with opposition. Did you continue doing what you knew God was calling you to do? Did you stray off course? What happened?

Rate yourself on the poverty-plateau-progress scale regarding the warfare test. Place an "X" at the place where you see your personal growth.

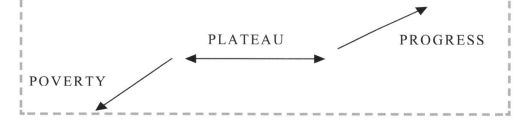

PLATEAU   PROGRESS

POVERTY

**God's Perspective:
Exodus 13.17-18**

"When Pharaoh finally let the people go, God did not lead them on the road that runs through Philistine territory, even though that was the shortest way from Egypt to the Promise Land. God said, "If the people are faced with battle, they might change their minds and return to Egypt. So God led them along a route through the wilderness toward the Red Sea, and the Israelites left Egypt like a marching army."

(NLT)

Esther 4.14

"If you keep quiet at a time like this, deliverance for the Jews will arise from some other place, but you and your relatives will die. What's more, who can say but that you have been elevated to the palace for just such a time as this."

(NLT)

John 15.16

"You didn't choose me. I chose you. I appointed you to go and produce fruit that will last, so that the Father will give you whatever you ask for, using My name."

(NLT)

Galatians 6.9

"So don't get tired of doing what is good. Don't get discouraged and give up, for we will reap a harvest of blessing at the appropriate time."

(NLT)

9. The test of time

This test proves the quality of our work; it is based on both opportunity and longevity.

Anyone can succeed for a short time, but a true leader's impact outlives him or her. As the saying goes, "Everyone has their fifteen minutes of fame," but a leader's work passes the test of time both in quality and endurance. This test also challenges our faithfulness to continue to do the right things even when we don't see immediate results.

This test evaluates us in **2** areas:

- Do we recognize and seize opportunities when they come?
- Does our life and leadership bear long lasting fruit?

real life...

Winston Churchill became prime minister in England at a perfect time for his style of leadership: World War II. He seized the moment. He called for courage from his people as he cried out against the Nazis. Later, we would observe this truth about all of us: "There comes a special moment in everyone's life. A moment for which that person is born. That special opportunity, when he seizes it, will fulfill his mission, a mission for which he is uniquely qualified. In that moment he finds his greatness. It is his finest hour."

reflect and respond... you

Are there opportunities in front of you right now that you fear the risk of seizing? Is God calling you to step out and take a risk?

What are you doing right now in your life that will still be important in twenty-five years?

What things can do to give permanence to your life?

People I can invest in: Opportunities I can pursue:

_____   _____

_____   _____

_____   _____

Rate yourself on the poverty-plateau-progress scale regarding the test of time. Place an "X" at the place where you see your personal growth.

PLATEAU   PROGRESS

POVERTY

10. The lordship test

This is a test revealing our heart's response to who or what has the final authority in our lives. It occurs in a situation where it becomes difficult to obey God.

It is likely that this test will come to us in the area of our strengths. God may choose to break us in a strength area. Jesus' close friend Peter had two strengths: one was his fishing ability and the other was his courage. Jesus tested both of these. Peter failed a test the night he boasted he would never deny Jesus and then did so three times. Fortunately, in Luke 5 he passed the test as he trusted Jesus instead of his expertise on fishing. In Luke 5.4-9, on the right, notice Peter's key words: "But if you say so..." He put God's word as His final authority.

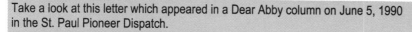

real life...

Take a look at this letter which appeared in a Dear Abby column on June 5, 1990 in the St. Paul Pioneer Dispatch.

Dear Abby:

    A young man from a wealthy family was about to graduate from high school. It was the custom in that affluent neighborhood for parents to give the graduate an automobile.

    Bill and his father had spent months looking at cars, and the week before graduation, they found the perfect car. Bill was certain that the car would be his on graduation night.

    Imagine his disappointment when, on the eve of his graduation, Bill's father handed him a gift-wrapped Bible!

    Bill was so angry that he threw the Bible down and stormed out of the house. He and his father never saw each other again.

    It was the news of his father's death that brought Bill home again. As he sat one night going through his father's possessions that he was to inherit, he came across the Bible his father had given him.

    He brushed away the dust and opened it to find a cashier's check, dated the day of his graduation — in the exact amount of the car they had chosen together.

reflect and respond...

Think about your own life. Are you willing to follow God even if He says something that doesn't seem logical or possible? Write about a time when you experienced the Lordship Test. What lessons did you learn? Did you pass the test?

Rate yourself on the poverty-plateau-progress scale regarding the lordship test. Place an "X" at the place where you see your personal growth.

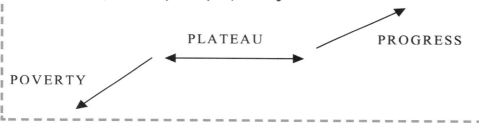

PLATEAU   PROGRESS

POVERTY

Whose strength will you rely on, yours or God's?

God's perspective:
Joshua 1.8
"Study this Book of the Law continually. Meditate on it day and night so that you may be sure to obey all that is written in it. Only then will you succeed."

(NLT)

Luke 5.4-9
When he had finished speaking, he said to Simon, "Now go out where it is deeper and let down your nets, and you will catch many fish." "Master," Simon replied, "we worked hard all last night and didn't catch a thing. But if you say so, we'll try again." And this time their nets were so full they began to tear! A shout for help bought their partners in the other boat, and soon both boats were filled with fish and on the verge of sinking. When Simon Peter realized what had happened, he fell to his knees before Jesus and said, "Oh, Lord, please leave me—I'm too much of a sinner to be around you." For he was awestruck by the size of their catch, as were the others with him.

(THE MESSAGE)

assess yourself...

A test is:
_____
_____

Go back and review each of the 10 tests. As you think about where you have been and where you are now, which tests have you faced in the past?

What tests are you currently facing?

This lesson was filled with opportunities to make changes in your life. Review any decisions or commitments you made and list them below.

Make sure that any decisions you made are followed by action. But remember, change takes time, it's a process. Be patient with yourself as you change and grow in light of God's grace.

bringing it all home...

"Search me, O God, and know my heart; test me and know my thoughts. Point out anything in me that offends you, and lead me along the path of everlasting life."

Psalm 139:23-24

behind *the scenes*

the personal life of a leader

The carnival was finally in town and David's dad had promised that today would be the day to go. David's anticipation level reached its peak as they waited in line at the ticket booth. Knowing the boy was bursting with energy, his dad sent him ahead to scope out the bustling activity awaiting them. When David's dad caught up with him, he was surprised to find the boy standing, mesmerized, in front of the "Guess-Your-Weight" scale. A very large man had just stepped onto the scales and was giving a great belly laugh as the operator gawked . . . the scales, apparently broken, were showing his weight to be only 75 pounds. David looked up at his father in complete amazement and exclaimed, "Look Dad, it's a hollow man!"

BASIC TRUTH

Taking responsibility in our personal lives will increase our ability to lead effectively

hollow people...

In reality, many of us live like hollow people. We look great on the outside but inside there is not much substance. How do we avoid this in an unbalanced, hectic world? It's often a battle just to keep the checkbook balanced, let alone our whole lives!

In this chapter, I want to offer a practical overview of the balanced personal life of a leader. This is not intended to be the ultimate solution for balance, but instead, it will allow us to take a step back and see the big picture of what a healthy leader looks like. I believe we must consistently balance four dimensions of our life: our responsibility to God, to others, to ourselves and to our call. Let's examine these here.

1. our responsibility to God

American Christians live with irony. We have become consumed with physical fitness, and therefore, we buy into a myriad of physical fitness plans. We've also become consumed with our spirituality, yet most people do not buy into any kind of spiritual "fitness" plan. We are spiritually undisciplined.

Perhaps the best picture of what is happening among Christians comes from the analogy of a wedding and marriage. Everyone understands that after every wedding comes a marriage. A healthy marriage requires an investment of time and energy. Likewise, in our Christian walk, after conversion comes a relationship that requires spiritual discipline. It feels like a marriage! We often put far too much emphasis on the wedding (our conversation) and not enough on the marriage (our discipline). Why do we need these disciplines in our lives? Because they restore in us God's…

- **Perspective:** balanced, "big picture" thinking"
- **Power:** resources and refreshment for the day
- **Purpose:** sense His mission and call on our lives
- **Peace:** poise and tranquility, even in outer turmoil
- **Presence:** experience of intimacy with Him

reflect and respond...

Describe your relationship with Christ right now. Do you see God's perspective, power, purpose, peace, and presence in your life? (Do you know you are doing what God has called you to do? Do you have peace about your calling and relationships? Do you often see things that cannot be explained apart from the presence of God?)

daily time...

So, how can we develop a spiritual "fitness" plan in our lives? How do we implement and maintain our spiritual disciplines? First, we must recognize that the development of a relationship takes time. We need to invest time daily with our Father in heaven. Does that seem overwhelming? Let's break it down. The following pages offer us a practical plan for personal time with God.

1. MAKE AN APPOINTMENT.

Decide on a time and a place to be alone with God. We must schedule it just as we do other "important" meetings. If Jesus did this, how much more do we need to? We should choose a time and place that best enables us to have uninterrupted blocks of time.

2. BEGIN BY BECOMING QUIET, THEN, ASK GOD TO SPEAK SPECIFICALLY.

Hearing God's voice is no accident. He speaks to us regularly, but we are not always listening. Remember young Samuel learning to hear God's voice (1 Samuel 3.1-10)? He came to know God because he demonstrated…

- Proper Practice—God speaks to those who obey what He has told them to do.
- Proper Proximity—God speaks to those who spend time in His presence.
- Proper Posture—God speaks to those who are quiet and still.

3. BRING THE RIGHT RESOURCES.

I believe the best times of meditation and personal study come when I have my Study Bible, a journal, a pen and sometimes a commentary or devotional guide as well. Don't be afraid to trade off. Try new resources to keep interaction fresh.

4. DEVELOP A GAME PLAN FOR STUDY.

We must prepare for meaningful conversation with God, just like we do with a person we love. We don't just barge in the door, run up to them and begin sharing meaningful, intimate words. It is the same with God. Perhaps we should start by reading a psalm to focus our minds on God —then ask God to speak to us. Next, we can determine the chapter or text we will focus on for the week. It is not wise to consistently approach the Bible by just flipping it open to a random passage. Our goal should be to get the whole counsel of God, so plan to read through an entire book of the Bible, even if it's one chapter at a time.

5. DETERMINE TO READ UNTIL A PRACTICAL PRINCIPLE OR TRUTH COMES ALIVE.

Most of us still read for "information" rather than "application." We must keep reading Scripture until we sense that God is sharing something with us personally. It is that "something" that can be carried with us throughout the day. Seizing one truth allows us to center on it. The adventure of discovery can be ours each time we approach God's Word. Clutching a truth we have not previously known (or practiced) is the discovery, and practicing that truth in life's "laboratory" is the adventure!

6. WRITE WHAT GOD IS SAYING THROUGH HIS WORD.

Whether or not we feel like writers, this is a solid discipline for all of us. People often experience a "wandering mind" syndrome during prayer, but writing has a unique ability to keep our thoughts on track. We also tend to forget God's activity in our lives. We learn lessons and experience the goodness of God, but it slips from our minds easily. Using a journal to write our thoughts provides a record of what God has taught us from week to week.

"God's word was not written to inform us but to transform us."

D.L. Moody

a model for **study...**

The following is a helpful pattern to use as we record the truths we learn from God's word. Simply jot a short paragraph, answering these three questions from the text.

DATE:
TEXT:
1. **"First Time" Meaning**
   (Write about what was happening or being spoken to the original audience.)
2. **"All-Time" Meaning**
   (Write about the all-time, universal truth of the passage. What is the principle?)
3. **"Now Time" Meaning**
   (Write about the application from the text for today. What should you do?)

7. LEARN TO MEDITATE ON THE SPECIFIC WORD THAT GOD HAS FOR YOU.

Once we have read the text and written its specific meaning and application for our own lives, it is helpful to **go back** and meditate on (even memorize) the specific verse(s) that God is using to speak to us. This is a practice that will allow the Holy Spirit to speak several things into our lives from a single passage! Note the difference between eastern and biblical meditation.

- **Eastern Meditation:** the emptying of oneself; it is an escape from the misery of the world's existence; detachment is the final goal of this mediation.
- **Biblical Meditation:** the filling of oneself with God, through His truth; it is the reflection of His word changing us from the inside out; attachment is the final goal of this meditation.

8. INTERNALIZE THE WORD THROUGH OBEDIENCE.

While scripture memorization is harder or easier for some, there is one sure-fire way to internalize the Bible. It isn't memorization cards with verses on them, or even setting the scripture to music (although both of these help!). It is a three-fold practice from the Bible itself, found in Ezra 7.10.

- STUDY IT
- PRACTICE IT
- SHARE IT

reflect and **respond...**

List any of the above activities that you feel challenged to begin doing in your life. How will you incorporate it? What do you hope to accomplish?

Key Principle:

Each scripture has one interpretation, but many applications.

2 Peter 1.19-21
James 1.22

2. our responsibility to others

the basics from the book...

Read Matthew 5.13-16
Jesus describes our role in the world in two ways. Fill in the blanks below.

"You are the _____ of the earth." (v.13)

"You are the _____ of the world." (v.14) (NIV)

reflect and respond...

What do these roles say about leadership? What do they say about your relationships?
What actions should you take to obey this command?

**God's perspective
Matthew 5.13-14**

You are the salt of the earth. But what good is salt if it has lost its flavor? Can you make it useful again? It will be thrown out and trampled underfoot as worthless. You are the light of the world—like a city on a mountain, glowing in the night for all to see.

(NLT)

me or you?

Every spiritual leader desiring to please God must value people. This is not an easy task. There are times when decisions are not black and white. In these times, the biggest temptation is to simply please yourself. Let me direct you to some wise counsel from the scriptures. When making decisions that involve others, we should use these guidelines. Read the text and see what God says. 1 CORINTHIANS 10.23-33

1. PRIORITIZE GOD'S PEOPLE (V.24-30)
We must put others first, especially if they are weaker and need our example.
Question: Do you keep others in mind when you choose your conduct? How?

2. PURSUE GOD'S GLORY (V.31)
Our chief goal is to glorify God in all we do and increase His reputation.
Question: In your decisions, do others get a clearer picture of who Christ is? In what ways?

3. PERCEIVE GOD'S PURPOSE (V.32-33)
God's ultimate purpose is to save everyone. He wants the world to know Him.
Question: Are your choices attracting others to or repelling others away from Jesus? Explain.

My network is my net worth...

You can tell a lot about yourself by identifying those who compose your "network." Complete the following diagram, developed by author Keith Drury, by inserting the names of people who affect the direction of your life. By seeing how your life is invested, and who influences you, you will better know what adjustments are necessary.

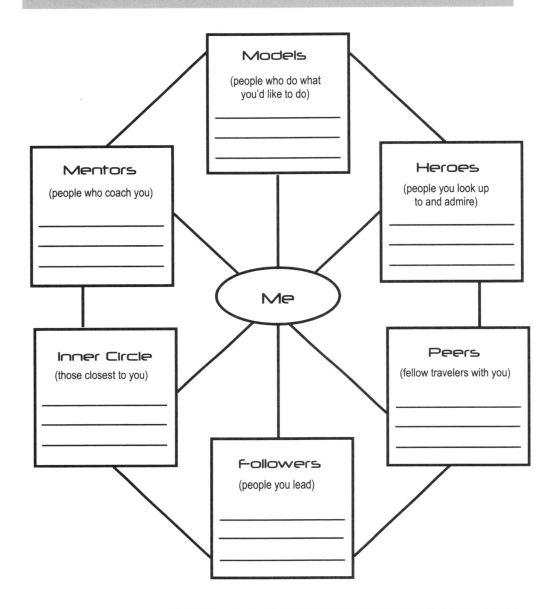

Opportunities did not always constitute a calling.

Needs did not always constitute a calling.

Burdens did not always constitute a calling.

Jesus...

When we consider our responsibilities in our relationship to others, we must look to the ultimate example, Jesus. Jesus never drifted from His mission as Leader and Savior, yet He also had time for people. God dictated His agenda, not people—but everyone felt empowered by Him. This is key. He only did what He saw the Father doing. He lived by His Father's bidding. Opportunities did not always constitute a calling. Needs did not always constitute a calling. Burdens did not always constitute a calling.

TRUTHS WE LEARN FROM JESUS AND HIS RELATIONSHIPS

- He was a faithful friend in the primary relationships of His life.

- He was a servant to everyone who had needs. He did what He could.

- He did not spend the same amount of time with all the disciples.

- He kept His relationship with His heavenly Father as the first priority.

how did he do that???

The Mode of Operation that Jesus embraced was quite simple. He never seemed rushed, yet He always seemed to get everything done. So what was His method? If you look at the big picture, Jesus' mode of operation can be simplified this way:

LOVE THE WORLD   MINISTER TO THE MANY   TRAIN THE FEW

It's very important to find a balance within the relationships of our lives because there are people always needing something from us. It can be very easy to forget the big picture. If we forget the ultimate goal, we will become slaves to the immediate circumstance. Jesus avoided this trap by allowing only His Father to dictate what He would do.

reflect and respond...

How does your life and leadership reflect Jesus' life and leadership? In one or two sentences, compare and contrast your style to His.

Jesus seemed to love the world, minister to the many and train the few. How have you done this?

rewind <<<

We've already looked at two areas of responsibility that a leader has in his or her personal life. Take a moment to review these areas and anything you have committed to change. Take some time to pray about your responsibilities and write your prayer below.

Love the World

Minister to the Many

Train the Few

 HALF TIME...continue the chapter next meeting

For us to be effective leaders, we must take care of our personal lives in four arenas. We have already looked at our responsibilities to God and to others and we have discussed how to balance them as Christ did. Now let's take a look at the last two arenas of responsibility.

3. our responsibility to ourselves

With so many areas of life clamoring for our attention, it's no wonder that we can easily overlook our personal needs. In fact, it's likely that at least one or more areas of our personal lives are neglected on a regular basis. Let's evaluate.

assess yourself...

Rate the following areas of your life on scale from 1 to 10. 1- completely neglected, 10 - perfectly healthy. Be honest with yourself.

Emotional Stability   _____

Physical Health and Fitness   _____

Sleep and Rest Patterns   _____

Spiritual Life   _____

Mental Stability   _____

Social and Relaxation Patterns   _____

reflect and respond...

Which area is your strongest? _____

Which area is your weakest? _____

What keeps your weak areas from being a perfect 10? (For example, I leave my studying to the last minute so sleep is neglected).

the balancing act...

Someone has said that life and leadership is a lot like juggling balls in the air. At first, it is fun and challenging to try and see how many you can keep in flight without dropping them. Then, you begin to realize that you can't do it, at least for very long. Suddenly, they begin to fall. As they do, you recognize that some of the balls are made of rubber, and they bounce right back. Others, however, are made of glass. They can break. In life and leadership, the challenge is to figure out which of yours are glass. I decided long ago that I could not drop my health or my family. Others seemed to bounce back and be OK if I dropped them once in a while.

Discuss the various balls you are juggling right now. Which ones are made of glass?

It begins with perspective...

So, how do we balance all of these areas of our personal life? Sometimes we feel pulled in so many directions that we don't even stop and take the time to think about it. The solution will come with a choice to be deliberate about what are priorities in our lives. As we evaluate our priorities, it is also extremely important to make sure that our perspective is right.

Three characteristics of a positive perspective for our personal lives

1. WHOLEHEARTEDNESS

Have you ever been in love? If you have, you know that it's an amazing feeling—a feeling that involves your *whole* heart. Can you imagine trying to fall in love in a half-hearted way? Of course not! It's a commitment and involvement on a deeper level. It is all or nothing!

involvement or commitment?

Years ago, there was a Kamikaze pilot who flew on 50 missions. Naturally, this was hard for people to understand. Kamikazes are supposed to give their life on the first flight they take, crashing into enemy buildings or ammunition compounds. A reporter asked the man, "How did you stay alive after flying on fifty suicide missions?" The pilot just smiled and said, "Well it's like this. I had a whole lot of involvement. Not much commitment...but a whole lot of involvement."

Sound familiar? Let's take a look at another perspective. Read 2 Chronicles 31.21.

Often in life we want to attempt things with only part of our heart. And, it's no wonder that we don't follow through—there is no commitment!

2 Chronicles 31.21

"In everything that he undertook in the service of God's temple and in obedience to the law and the commands, he sought his God and worked wholeheartedly. And so he prospered."

NIV

115

2. SINGLE-MINDEDNESS

Think again about falling in love. In order to give our "whole heart" it must be devoted to one thing. Imagine falling in love with several people at the same time? It just wouldn't work. In the same way, we must devote our minds and thoughts to a single focus. The key is keeping perspective. This is not to imply that we will only think about one thing all the time. Instead, we are to keep our **dominant** focus on one thought—the foundation for all other things.

what perspective should we have???

- Jesus is coming
  - Read 2 Peter 3.10
- Life is short
  - Read James 4.14
- Labor is not in vain
  - Read 1 Corinthians 15.58

God's Perspective

Hebrews 12.2

"Let us fix our eyes on Jesus, the author and perfecter of our faith."

(NIV)

3. PASSION

We have already established that falling in love requires a wholehearted commitment and a single-minded perspective, but there is still something missing: Passion. Passion is the fire behind love, it is truly an essential element.

Think about it. If you needed to heat your apartment, would you light a candle or start a fire in the fireplace? Obvious answer, isn't it? In the same way that a small amount of fire creates a small amount of heat, a small amount of passion creates a small result!

reflect and respond...

Wholeheartedness: List three things that you wish to wholeheartedly develop in your life right now. List a practical step for each that you will take.

Single-mindedness: What things usually dominate your focus? What changes do you need to make to develop a single-minded perspective?

Passion: What things are you passionate about? Are you actively working in those areas of passion?

4. our responsibility to our calling

The final factor in the equation is our responsibility to the calling placed on our lives. God calls each of us to specific roles, based on who he created us to be. We are responsible to respond to this calling based on our unique gifts and talents. Once we recognize the balance between God, others, and self we can evaluate the fruit of it all. The fruit is what God says must be inspected—it is how we live the life and what we produce after all is said and done. We are called to be ministers of God wherever we are.

case study: samson

Samson was a judge in the Old Testament. He will always be remembered for his brute strength. But this external strength was masking significant internal weakness. We might say he had a strong bicep but a weak backbone. He failed to develop convictions where he needed them as a leader. Notice the signals of weakened leadership from his life, in Judges 14-16.

Leaders without convictions can often be identified this way...

1. They have not addressed glaring weaknesses in their character.

2. They count on deception to safeguard themselves.

3. They are impetuous and act on a whim or impulse.

4. They play games with their place of influence.

5. They can be deceived, especially in their blind spots.

6. They are prone to misuse their God-given gifts.

7. They can be bought.

reflect and respond...

1. Is their any part of your life that mirrors Samson's?

2. How have you been tempted in the past and needed convictions in your leadership?

UNDERSTANDING CONVICTIONS...

What is a conviction?

A principle you are so committed to practicing and believing in that you not only live for it, but you will die for it. It is a part of who you are.

Now is the time to build convictions in your life. Convictions are stronger than ideas. In fact, notice the order of strength in the list below.

1. **IDEAS AND THOUGHTS** – May come and go every week of our life.
2. **PREFERENCES AND OPINIONS** – A bit stronger, but still may change often.
3. **FEELINGS AND COMPULSIONS** – Stronger still, and involve our emotions.
4. **COMMITMENTS AND DECISIONS** – Even stronger, and involve our minds.
5. **CONVICTIONS AND VALUES** – Strongest, involving mind, will and emotion.

building convictions...

Convictions come in our lives when...

1. We have studied and learned what God's Word says on a given subject.

2. We choose to apply and obey the Word in everyday life contexts.

3. We have exposed ourselves repeatedly to a need in that area.

4. We meditate on specific truths over a period of six months to a year.

5. We have decided what is worth living and dying for.

6. We associate with people who possess convictions in the same areas.

7. We have settled the issue before we are forced to do so.

reflect and respond...

Do you have any convictions already established in your life? If so, what are they?

What are some convictions you want to build into your life and leadership?

How will you build them?

questions to ask ourselves

What do I feel God is calling me to do?

What are my spiritual gifts and personality traits?

Am I at peace with who I am?

!! success !!

When we understand who we are and what we are called to be, we need to evaluate how we will be successful in those areas. What does success really mean?

- Knowing my calling/purpose.
- Growing towards my potential.
- Sowing seeds of success in the lives of others.

reflect and respond...

What do you sense God is calling you do in your own life?

Are you living your calling?

take another look

As Christian leaders we must be good stewards of the gifts that He has given us. It's important that we find balance in our personal lives. However, if we are not careful, the concept of balance can become the end in itself rather than the means to a healthy lifestyle. The following pages contain an article by Paul Stanley that offers an excellent perspective on the concept of balance.

the myth of the balanced life:
an alternative view

By Paul Stanley

I've met believers who are models of the "balanced life." Their giving flows out of beautifully balanced budgets and their lifestyles include all the right activities to develop balance. Their priorities undergo tough appraisal to ensure they are "properly" weighted. Even their service to Christ is balanced to carefully include "enough but not too much."

But I wonder: Are people who strive for balance in their lives following Christ, or a value system concocted by the elusive "experts"? Have we elevated "balance" to a place never intended in scripture?

Jesus: A Life Out Of Balance

Under the commonly held concept of the balanced life, Jesus was often out of balance. He missed meals, worked long hours, and seemed to have many short nights. We find Jesus getting up early to pray when He probably could have used the sleep (Mark 1:35). He even spent forty days praying and fasting, to the point that the angels had to minister to Him.

Yet as we read through the gospels, we don't get the impression that Jesus was always pressing Himself and His disciples to the outer limits, continually neglecting physical rest and nourishment. It is interesting to note that it was Christ- not the disciples- who was concerned about the hungry five thousand.

How did Jesus decide when it was time to minister and when to rest? His statement in John 4 gives us a clue.

Jesus and his disciples, on the way form Judea to Galilee, were tired and hungry when they stopped in a small Samaritan village. Yet Jesus set aside His needs in order to lead an adulterous Samaritan woman to the "Living Water." As His disciples joined Him by the town well, they were concerned about His need to eat, but He wasn't. Christ responded, "My food is to do the will of Him who sent me and to finish His work" (John 4:34).

Jesus determined when to eat and when to abstain, when to work and when to rest by seeking His Father's guidance. Christ's drive wasn't to achieve balance, but to do the will of the Father.

Out Of Control

Sensitivity to the Holy Spirit, not a conceived "yardstick," must determine our priorities as well. The goal in life is never "balance" but rather doing God's will to the fullest, with all the energy and time God gives us. Like Jesus, we too will sometimes devote a disproportionate amount of energy to one area as we listen and obey His Spirit.

God never intended for us to live "balanced" lives, with all aspects under control. While we may prefer to live within self-defined boundaries that allow us to be safe and in control, following Christ often requires more risk. We need to be willing to be "out of balance" so Christ can lead and use us where He wants us.

Faith begins to grow when we sacrifice something in our monthly budget to give a little more than last month, especially when it is focused on a need the Spirit has revealed. Dependence on Christ's power meets blessing when we step beyond our comfort zone and give time and love to people around us... even when it takes resources we may not think we have or time we've intended to devote elsewhere. It seems that most of the work of the Kingdom is done by overworked believers with average gifts and few earthly resources. Perhaps these laborers don't know about balance yet.

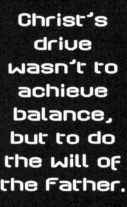

Christ's drive wasn't to achieve balance, but to do the will of the Father.

Whose Agenda?

Spending years with the Eastern European and Soviet believers changed my life in the area of balance. They were always "out of balance" by anyone's measure. Food supplies were erratic, persecution was unpredictable, and change was constant. As a result, they did not worry about tomorrow but focused on fulfilling His will today. They knew God would take care of the rest.

And He did! None of them ever starved (though they often ate a lot of one food). They had adequate clothing. But, most of all, God was powerfully working in and through them. Always giving and sharing, these believers saw God answer prayer, change lives, and fulfill promises.

The apostle Paul challenged the Ephesians (5.15-18) to live wisely, "making the most of every opportunity"; not to be foolish, but to "understand what the Lord's will is." If we worry and think too much about "balance," it is easy to fall into an agenda that stifles the Spirit's prompting.

Somehow, we must trust that God is at work in us and that the way He is moving in our lives is part of a larger movement in the world. As we respond to His Spirit, God reveals to us the steps we are to take toward fulfilling His will…and this may pull our lives out of balance. Very often it is in these "out of balance times" and circumstances that God teaches us new and vital lessons because He has our attention. After all, when do we call upon the "Wonderful Counselor, Mighty God, Everlasting Father, and Prince of Peace"? When we are "out of balance." He also works through us because our faith is alive and we are thrust into dependence on Him (2 Corinthians 12:10). His power shows up best in weak people.

Let's model our lives after those who followed Christ in the New Testament. They abandoned to God's will at any cost and allowed God the freedom to pull them out of balance anytime. As a matter of fact, they anticipated it. Most of their lives were spent drawing upon Christ in their "out-of-balance-yet-in-His-will" state. True growth and adventure with Christ take place in "out of balance" living.

Here's wishing you a wonderful out-of-balance life!

reflect and respond...

What did you learn from this article? Write about any thoughts or ideas that were outstanding to you.

In this chapter, we have discussed how to bring balance to our personal lives as leaders. How do you reconcile this idea of living a balanced life with Paul Stanley's point that Jesus lived an out of balanced life? Do you agree or disagree with him?

assess yourself...

It is easy to become consumed with the idea of "spirituality" or to maintain an appearance of being spiritual, but behind the scenes, we lack the disciplines that develop our spiritual life. Review the steps for developing a spiritual "fitness" plan. Which are currently a part of your life? Which do you need to begin doing? What changes will you make in your life to being implementing these? Write out the practical steps you will take to do so.

In looking at our responsibility to others, we see that Jesus had a very simple Mode of Operation: love the world, minister to the many, train the few. How will you adopt this Mode of Operation? Specifically, how can you love the world, minister to the many, and train the few?

It is true that while there are many good and worthwhile things to involve ourselves in, we need to limit ourselves to what is best—what fits best with our unique gifts and passions. After evaluating yourself in the areas of wholeheartedness, single-mindedness, and passion, what will you do to narrow the priorities in your life to maintain a more balanced personal life. What do you need to cut out? What do you need to focus more attention on?

A conviction is:

_____

What are you willing to die for? Do you find yourself lacking in conviction? How will you keep yourself from becoming a leader like Samson?

bringing it all home...

Robert Frost was awaiting admittance, many, many years ago, into a student fraternity and was told confidentially that only one factor was delaying his entry: the fact that he took long walks in the woods by himself. In other words, America's future poet was caught red-handed engaging in solitude. He was caught being an individual, with an inner life of his own, instead of the dead and public machine life of joining a crowd in a movie or around a radio. When they asked him what he did while walking alone in the woods, Robert Frost was not so foolish as to admit the truth that he was guilty of writing poetry there. Instead, he saved the day and won his fraternity acceptance by replying: "Gnawing the bark off trees."

"The fight is for the private life. The over adjusted man knows only the public life. Three of the differing modes of creativity — religious, aesthetic, intellectually — have this in common: They are what the individual does with his aloneness." — Peter Viereck

Congratulations! You have just completed the first step in the journey of becoming a more effective leader. We hope that you have gained new insights into yourself and a better understanding of leadership. But don't stop here!

take the next step...

This workbook is part of a series of six workbooks on leadership. Over the series you will study and discuss the spiritual formation, the skill formation, and the strategic formation of a leader. At EQUIP, we want to encourage you to begin the next workbook in the series! To learn more about EQUIP, please turn the page.

We would also like to know who you are! It is our desire to help in adding to your leadership ability by keeping you posted on what is happening in leadership.

to contact us or to place an order:

call toll free: 888-993-7847, extension 3311

or visit our website: www.equiporg.org

a little more about EQUIP...

EQUIP is a non-profit Christian organization devoted to the development of Christ-like leaders in the most influential and neglected places of our world. We believe that everything rises and falls on leadership. We partner with ministries, churches, and schools in three key areas: the international community, the urban community, and the academic community. This workbook is part of our partnership in the academic arena.

Developing leaders in the academic community allows us to invest in tomorrow's leaders today. Here are at a few of the resources that we currently offer...

- **Leadership Conferences**

  The *Leadership Forums* are 1-2 day training events tailor-made to the needs of your campus ministry. They can be profiled as outreach events on your campus for fraternities, sororities, RA's, student government, etc. The conferences serve as a catalyst to build hunger for further personal leadership development.

- **Mentoring Groups**

  The *Leadership Exchange* contains a year's worth of leadership cassette tapes, taught by Dr. John C. Maxwell, to spark discussion and application in monthly mentoring groups. In addition to the tapes, student handbooks and facilitator's guides are provided. Along with this, we offer "Portrait of a Leader," a series of six discussion guides on leadership. Our hope is to provide support, interaction, accountability, and to foster a leadership culture within your ministry through these tools.

- **Video Curriculum**

  The *Leadership Journey* is designed to furnish ongoing, systematic leadership training for students. The video curriculum is divided into 72 12-minute segments to be viewed in class, and then discussed. The lectures cover the 21 Irrefutable Laws of Leadership and are taught by Dr. John C. Maxwell and Dr. Tim Elmore. It is crafted to be used in a classroom setting along with assignments and reading.

- **Resources**

  The *Leadership Library* represents a fourth component in our partnership. EQUIP offers a battery of books, tapes, videos, and training manuals for leaders and potential leaders to enhance your leadership growth. The resources cover subjects including leadership, mentoring, spiritual growth, people skills, priorities, vision, staff development, and more. These have been discounted for campus workers and students.